ADVANCE PRAISE

"An accessible, sensible introduction to the theory of ecopsychology and the methods of ecotherapy. Recommended for both therapists and for anyone interested in the human–nature connection."
— **Howard Frumkin, MD, DrPH,** emeritus professor and former dean, University of Washington School of Public Health, and former director, National Center for Environmental Health, U.S. Centers for Disease Control and Prevention

"This is a timely and much-needed volume, grounded in the understanding that humans are connected to the natural world. Drawing on research, history, and personal experience, Hasbach provides both theoretical support and practical suggestions for a therapeutic approach that supports psychological well-being by helping people recognize that connection as part of their identity. A must read for nature-informed mental health care."
— **Susan Clayton, PhD,** Whitmore-Williams Professor of Psychology, The College of Wooster

"As the evidence continues to mount on the benefits of connecting deeply to the natural world, here comes Patricia Hasbach's indispensable guide for clinicians, patients, and all of us. This is the book we need right now."
— **Florence Williams,** author of *The Nature Fix* and *Heartbreak: A Personal and Scientific Journey*

"Patricia Hasbach is a pioneering voice for ecotherapy and ecopsychology. In recent years, a growing body of scientific evidence shows that people of all ages are suffering physically, psychologically, and spiritually from a disconnection from the natural world. For many, that disconnect is a matter of life and death. To this cause, Hasbach brings not only her clinical expertise but also the voice of her heart. *Prescribing Nature* is a seminal work and a milestone for the new nature movement."

—**Richard Louv,** author of *Last Child in the Woods: Saving Our Children from Nature-Deficit Disorder*

PRESCRIBING

NATURE

PRESCRIBING
NATURE

A Clinician's Guide
to Ecotherapy

PATRICIA H. HASBACH, PhD

Norton Professional Books

An Imprint of W. W. Norton & Company
Independent Publishers Since 1923

Note to Readers: This book is intended as a general information resource for professionals practicing in the field of psychotherapy and mental health. It is not a substitute for appropriate training or clinical supervision. Standards of clinical practice and protocol vary in different practice settings and change over time. No technique or recommendation is guaranteed to be safe or effective in all circumstances, and neither the publisher nor the author(s) can guarantee the complete accuracy, efficacy, or appropriateness of any particular recommendation in every respect or in all settings or circumstances.

Any URLs displayed in this book link or refer to websites that existed as of press time. The publisher is not responsible for, and should not be deemed to endorse or recommend, any website other than its own or any content that it did not create. The author, also, is not responsible for any third-party material.

For those who bring hope and inspiration into the world

CONTENTS

ACKNOWLEDGMENTS

I am very grateful to Deborah Malmud, vice president at W. W. Norton & Company and publishing director of Norton Professional Books, for recognizing the potential of the emerging practice of ecotherapy and reaching out to me. Our initial discussions about ecopsychology and nature-based therapy led to the opportunity to write this book. I also want to thank my editor Jamie Vincent and all those at Norton Professional Books for their work that brought this book to its current form including McKenna Tanner, Irene Vartanoff, and Mariah Eppes.

I want to thank the many patients who have shared a portion of their life journey with me over the years. I have enormous gratitude for their trust in the process and in our therapeutic relationship.

I am grateful for the graduate school training I received in counseling psychology at the University of Pittsburgh—especially from the late Joseph Werlinich and Judith Scott. Who I am as a therapist was born, nurtured, and developed in the master's and doctoral programs there. A decade into my private practice, I was introduced to the new field of ecopsychology. Wanting to learn all that was available then, I pursued another master's degree at Naropa University, which had one of the few programs that offered an ecopsychology concentration. My thanks to the faculty in the MATP program, especially John Davis and Jed Swift, whose guidance deepened my exploration of ecopsychology.

I want to express my gratitude for those who have supported me as a writer. My coeditor, Peter Kahn, and the contributors to *The Rediscovery of the Wild* and *Ecopsychology: Science, Totems, and the Technological Species* helped me find my own voice as a writer in the creation of both of those volumes. The more recent publication of *Grounded* challenged me to write for a nonacademic audience. Dinah Dunn and her team at Indelible Editions provided valuable guidance and support. I am grateful to Deborah Malmud and Jamie Vincent for reviewing early chapters of this book. Their enthusiastic support fueled my confidence and commitment to see it through to completion. I also want to express my sincere appreciation to Richard Louv and the late Barry Lopez for discussions that provided inspiration and continue to influence my thoughts and my writing.

I also want to express my deep appreciation for the colleagues in this field who came before me. Their pioneering spirit and deep insights inform my work every day. I'm also deeply grateful for the colleagues whose work continues to shape the field of ecopsychology and contributes to the growth and development of nature-based methods for a variety of client populations and settings.

This book could not have been written without the work of the researchers who have provided the evidence that supports ecotherapy as a best practice in today's world. Their work demonstrates the importance of nature to humans' health and well-being and is illuminating the psychological impacts of climate change that we must address as mental health providers.

When one puts their life on hold to write a book while continuing their day job, there are many people that hold space, offer support, and extend grace. I am especially grateful to my dear friends: Mary Anne Basilone, Linda Potter, Jo Johnston, and Randy and Lo Lewis. I'm appreciative of the love and support I received from my family. Alex, Kayla, and little Alder James represent hope for the future. A special thanks goes out to my husband, Thomas Hasbach, who picked up a lot of extra household work, read every word of this manuscript, and offered valuable suggestions, and extended loving support throughout the process.

Finally, I want to express my deep gratitude for the continued sense of belonging, joy, and wonder provided by my home place. I am so fortunate to be surrounded by nature's beauty every day. It is that love for the natural world that inspires me to do all I can to advocate for its care and protection.

PREFACE

My journey into the practice of ecotherapy began in the 1990s in an outdoor courtyard of a community hospital's cardiac rehab center. New to private practice, I consulted with the cardiac rehabilitation department on patients who had difficulty engaging in their physical rehab program because of psychological concerns like anxiety and depression. At that time, we were just beginning to understand the social and emotional aspects of recovery from a cardiac event. One afternoon I was scheduled to meet with a new patient who was particularly resistant to the idea of talking with a counselor or therapist. From his perspective, it was his heart that failed him, not his mind. From information on the patient chart, I learned that he was the owner of a landscaping business. When I met him in my private corner of the rehab center, I could tell he was anxious. Intuitively, I sensed he was much more comfortable outdoors, so I suggested we take a walk out to the newly created courtyard that was adjacent to the rehab center. As we walked the short, curving path through the courtyard, he noticed the newly planted shrubs and young trees and commented on several of them. I asked him how he got involved with landscaping and gardening and he began to tell his story. As we sat on one of the outdoor benches, he was visibly more relaxed as he talked about his work and his love of plants, birds, and pollinators. His speech slowed, his breathing steadied, and he stopped wringing his hardworking hands. By the end of our session, he had shared his fear that he might never be able to do the physical work he could do prior to his heart attack. The spontaneous outdoor session I had with this patient became an "aha" moment for me. The surrounding nature brought something special to our time together.

Since then, much has been learned about the impact of nature on the therapeutic process. *Prescribing Nature: A Clinician's Guide to Ecotherapy* is written for mental health practitioners (psychologists, counselors, and social workers), as well as students in those fields, who would like to incorporate the natural world into their work. Traditionally, therapy occurs in indoor office spaces and focuses on human-to-human relationships and issues that stop at the urban boundary. But with a robust body of evidence that direct contact with nature has powerful psychological and emotional benefits, and a growing awareness of the psychological impacts of climate change, many clinicians are interested in adding ecotherapy to their clinical toolbox.

I wrote this book because I recognize the need for a practical "how to" guide on the nature-based methods of ecotherapy that is relevant and accessible for today's busy practitioner. During my three decades as a private practice clinician, I've spent many hours working with clients inside and outside the office setting. I have seen the profound impact of nature engagement on the therapeutic process. Ecotherapy offers a systematic way to think about incorporating nature into treatment planning, as well as specific tools to speak about the distress of climate change and its impact on human and planetary health. I have also worked with hundreds of graduate students interested in learning about ecopsychology and the nature-based methods of ecotherapy. I've heard their questions, seen their excitement, and felt their overwhelm as they navigate the numerous methods they are exposed to in graduate school. But one consistent comment I hear from students is that ecotherapy is so relevant today.

In each chapter, I've included research that provides evidence for the efficacy of the therapeutic practices described. Intuitively, we know that engaging with nature is good for us. In the last few years there has been an explosion of new research that makes the case for the importance of nature in our lives. *Prescribing Nature: A Clinician's Guide to Ecotherapy* provides the reader with the theoretical grounding for the practice of ecotherapy and offers specific practices the clinician can utilize to deepen their work and broaden the scope of treatment to include the human–nature relationship. It is my hope that this book will be a valuable resource for today's mental health providers.

PRESCRIBING

NATURE

PART I

Overview

1

INTRODUCTION
TO ECOTHERAPY

Twenty years ago, my family and I moved into our home in paradise. Situated in western Oregon in the foothills of the Cascades, on the shores of the McKenzie River, this place fulfilled a dream to live in the west. We were surrounded by fresh air, tall Douglas firs, and the constant sound of whitewater on the McKenzie. Our neighbors included an osprey pair that nested across the river every spring, bald eagles that competed with the osprey for salmon and steelhead, deer that wandered through my gardens regularly, elk that came down from the mountains to the river in winter, and cougar that left prints at the water's edge. We remodeled the house, planted thriving gardens (much to the deer's delight), and paddled on the river every chance we got. Each day began with a deep sense of gratitude for this special place we now called home. There were no worries of wildfires then.

All that changed in the fall of 2020, when the Holiday Farm Fire swept through the McKenzie Valley and burned 173,393 acres before it was extinguished. We fled from our home in the middle of the night under a Level 3 evacuation order ("Leave Now") with our two pups, the contents of a safe, and the clothes we were wearing. For fourteen days, we wondered if we would have a home to return to. Firefighters from multiple states and Canada as well as the National Guard were mobilized to fight the blaze that now ranks among one of Oregon's biggest fires in state history. We were among the fortunate. Our home, though damaged, was still standing thanks to the heroic efforts of firefighters and first responders. But many residents in the McKenzie Valley were not so lucky. Over 700 homes and businesses were lost, and one person died. The osprey family lost their nesting snag—evidence of its charred trunk remains in the river. No elk have been seen at the river's edge, and the landscape across the river is no longer a lush green forest. Today, like so many, we live with the constant threat of wildfire during an ever extending fire season. We are better prepared than we were during that frightful night. But the anxiety remains.

In the aftermath of the fire, I heard many stories of escape, loss, fear, and disorientation by my clients. Many of them chose to live in this wilder environ to be in deep communion with the natural world. My knowledge and skills as an ecopsychologist helped me understand and navigate the emotion-filled waters that the people of my community were experiencing.

Many clinicians are unprepared to address the deep emotions connected with the rapidly changing environment. Our training focuses on intrapsychic processes and human-to-human relationships: interpersonal relationships, family relationships, and interactions with society and culture. Most training programs in counseling and psychology do not address an environment in crisis or the mental health issues related to it. The theoretical foundations of ecopsychology and the practice of ecotherapy expand the context of care to include the human–nature relationship. This emerging field is beginning to address the complex systems of the environment, economics, and related politics that affect us all as a species. Ecotherapy recognizes that the climate crisis has deep psychological and social implications: the acute trauma of living through climate disasters, the ongoing fear of a collapsing ecosystem, and the psychosocial impacts to communities affected by climate disruption.

Not only does ecotherapy address the emotions and trauma of climate-related disasters, but also it recognizes the many benefits of nature connection in our lives. There is a solid and expansive body of evidence that supports the assertion that interacting with nature is good for our psychological and emotional health.

Our species came of age embedded in and interacting with nature, which has shaped the human psyche and nurtured our body, mind, and soul. What we intuitively know about the healing benefits of nature interaction is now supported by robust research that paves the way for clinicians to incorporate the natural world into their therapeutic work as a best practice.

Current research demonstrates that interacting with nature can lower stress levels, decrease anxiety symptoms, and reduce ruminations of depression, as well as symptoms associated with ADHD in children. Studies suggest that our relationship with nature may be deeply linked to our sense of happiness and well-being, indicating the relationship plays an important role in maintaining positive mental health. Exposure to nature has been shown to hasten recovery from surgery, boost productivity and job satisfaction, increase creativity, and improve cognitive function.

Prescribing Nature: A Clinician's Guide to Ecotherapy is written for mental health professionals who would like to incorporate the natural world into their work with clients. Traditionally, therapy occurs in indoor office spaces and focuses on issues that stop at the urban boundary, a human-centric approach. But with a growing awareness of the impacts of climate-related anxiety and trauma, and mounting evidence that direct contact with nature has powerful psychological and emotional benefits, there is a growing interest in the field of ecopsychology and the practice of ecotherapy. This book discusses the theoretical foundations of ecotherapy and its many applications and offers specific practices clinicians can add to their therapeutic toolbox to deepen their work and broaden the lens of therapy to include the human–nature relationship.

A FEW DEFINITIONS

Clinebell (1996) was the first to use the term *ecotherapy* in his pioneering book, *Ecotherapy: Healing Ourselves, Healing the Earth*. He defined ecotherapy as "the healing and growth that is nurtured by healthy interactions with the earth" (p. xxi). In the edited volume, *Ecotherapy: Healing with Nature in Mind*, Buzzell and Chalquist (2009) defined ecotherapy as "an umbrella term for nature-based methods for physical and psychological healing . . . that acknowledges the vital role of nature and addresses the human–nature relationship" (p. 18). Some authors refer to ecotherapy not only as an expansion of psychotherapy into the natural environment, but as a *cultural movement* to heal the separation between humans and nature. These definitions have all contributed to the evolution of the emerging field of ecopsychology and the practice of ecotherapy.

In this book, I define ecotherapy with a more precise definition, using a clinical lens. I recognize and respect that others may hold a broader view. As a clinician, I want to foster a definition of ecotherapy that allows its methods to be tested in order to demonstrate ecotherapy's effectiveness as a therapeutic modality, so that it can stand alongside other therapies in the clinician's toolbox such as cognitive–behavioral therapy, family systems therapy, relationship therapy, and so on. I define *ecotherapy* as a therapeutic modality that expands the scope of treatment to include humans' relationship with the natural world of which we are a part.

I also want to clarify how I am defining *nature* in this volume. According to the *Oxford English Dictionary*, nature as a noun is defined as "the phenomena of the physical world collectively, including plants, animals, the landscape, and other features and products of the earth, as opposed to humans or human creations." A review of several other dictionary definitions of nature reveals some confusion as to whether humans are included in the definition of nature or not. This duality of humans as separate from the natural world is at the heart of the disconnection experienced by so many people in our modern society, leading to a plethora of physical and psychological problems. For this book, I am defining nature as the physical world and all that exists that is not human built (e.g., plants, animals, birds, insects, amphibians, mountains, oceans, lakes, rivers, forests, the stars of the universe, and yes, humans). I also recognize that nature exists on a continuum of domestic nature (e.g., a backyard garden or urban park) to wild nature (e.g., a vast ocean or a mountain landscape). I make the assumption that therapeutic work can happen in all these environments.

NOVEL PRACTICE OR ANCIENT WISDOM?

Interacting with nature for mental health and well-being isn't new. Ancestral healers have suggested interactions with various elements of nature since the dawn of human civilization. Shamans, elders, guides, and medicine women and men incorporated nature's healing powers into the performance of ritual and ceremony to mark rites of passage, help people recover from illness, let go of a painful event, and cope with the unknown.

Early healers from around the world believed that nature held an energy, a life force, which could be transferred to people to promote health and well-being. Records show that early Roman physicians believed that walking in gardens, being by water, and exposure to natural light all contributed to improved mental health.

During the mid-19th century, medical doctors prescribed time in the Alps in Europe and in the Adirondacks in the United States to address multiple afflictions and mental health concerns related to the Industrial Revolution. A thriving industry of medical sanitariums and health resorts grew to offer a natural retreat from the stresses of modern civilization. As the authors of *Your Brain on Nature* point out, this practice was not based on scientific evidence, but was a return to the intuitive recommendations of the ancient healers (Selhub & Logan, 2012).

Carl Jung, the Swiss psychiatrist and psychoanalyst who founded analytical psychology, incorporated nature into his work with his patients, recognizing that our inner world and the outer world are connected. In *Memories, Dreams, Reflections* (1957/1989), Jung describes the interconnectedness he personally experienced. It is a stunning example of what ecopsychology today refers to as the *ecological unconscious*:

At times I feel as if I am spread out over the landscape and inside things, and am myself living in every tree, in the splashing of the waves, in the clouds and the animals that come and go, in the procession of the seasons. There is nothing . . . with which I am not linked. (p. 225)

Jung viewed dreams and the psychic depths as nature. In *Dream Analysis* (1984*)*, he wrote "Walking in the woods, lying in the grass, taking a bath in the sea are from the outside; entering the unconscious, entering yourself through dreams, is touching nature from the inside and this is the same thing, things are put right again" (p. 142).

Intuitively, the healers of old knew that time spent in the outdoors, in direct contact with the natural world, was good medicine.

RATIONALE FOR THE PRACTICE OF ECOTHERAPY

From an evolutionary perspective, we need a relationship with the natural world to fully flourish as human beings. But with our urban, industrialized, technological culture, we are living further removed from the natural world than any time in our species' history. It is estimated that by 2050, 70% of the world's population will live in urban centers. The average adult currently spends more than 93% of their time indoors (Bratman et al., 2015), often in front of a screen. A 2019 Neilson report found that the average adult spent 11.5 hours each day consuming media. Half of the 18–29-year-olds surveyed that same year by the Pew Research Center said they were online almost constantly. Studies by the Kaiser Foundation tell us that in 2010, children ages 8–18, spent on average 7.5 hours each day engaged with some sort of screen for entertainment and only 4–7 minutes each day in unstructured outdoor play (Rideout et al., 2010). A follow-up study found that the time spent in front of a screen increased to 9.9 hours in 2016, and this did not include computer time at school or doing homework. We can safely assume that since the pandemic, those screen time hours have likely increased again.

With competition for our time and attention, less exposure to nature may undermine our connection with, and appreciation of, the natural world. For instance, in a study of 16,000 people in England who said they do not visit natural environments regularly, 22% reported that they were "not interested," felt that time in nature was "not for people like them," or reported "no particular reason" for not visiting nature (Boyd et al., 2018).

It is quite possible for today's child to grow up without ever having taken a solitary walk in the woods or spent time foraging for pine cones, leaves, flowers, or rocks—precious treasures. Imagine never experiencing the quiet of nature, interrupted only by the calls of birds, the rush of a stream, or the rustling of leaves in the wind. Imagine never seeing a night sky full of stars. We know the territory that today's children can freely explore outdoors is a fraction of that which their parents and grandparents could roam. As we lose our intimate affiliation with nature and accept diminished experiences as the norm, we are also losing a considerable range of human feelings: the joy and delight of discovery, the sense of adventure, the experience of awe, the feeling of belonging to something bigger than ourselves, and the humility that comes in the presence of wildness. The educator and author, Robert Michael Pyle (1993), called this phenomenon the "extinction of experience." With an intentional focus on the human–nature relationship, ecotherapy can address these essential interactions that many people are losing and encourage a reconnecting of ourselves to the natural world.

In calling for the protection of wild places, author Terry Tempest Williams states, " . . . our capacity to face the harsh measures of life comes from the deep quiet of listening to the land, the river, the rocks. There is a humility that has evolved with the earth. It is best retrieved in solitude . . . " (2001, p. 17). She speaks beautifully of the natural parallel between inner and outer wildness.

In my clinical practice, I notice that clients who have been invited to take their reflective work outdoors either during a session or as a homework assignment begin to map inner experiences onto natural phenomenon. Or, said another way, they describe their inner experience using metaphors from nature. An example of this mapping is a man who describes feeling numb to his feelings, then allows himself to set foot into a cold mountain stream and describes the feeling as one of waking up. Another example is a teen who describes himself as bored with everything. When asked about one time he remembers feeling alive and engaged, he describes a fishing trip. His nature prescription becomes going fishing one time with a buddy. Weeks later, he was still going out to a nearby fishing hole after school—sometimes alone. During our sessions, he was able to express more feelings about a family situation that left him feeling adrift and alone. These nature mappings provide a resource to mine for deeper understandings.

Our dissociation from the natural world also comes with health-related costs. The popular author and founder of the Children & Nature Network, Richard Louv (2008), coined the term "nature deficit disorder" to describe the health and behavioral problems that can result from the decrease in contact with nature so prevalent today. The U.S. Department of Health & Human Services states that between 13% and 20% of children living in the United States experience a mental disorder each year, with the prevalence of these conditions increasing. Nearly 10 million children in the United States are being prescribed stimulants for ADHD, antidepressants, antianxiety medications, and other psychotropic drugs (Howie et al., 2014).

In 2021, an estimated 21 million adults aged 18 years or older in the United States reported that they had at least one major depression episode in the past year. The prevalence of major depressive episodes was highest among individuals age 18–25 years (Substance Abuse and Mental Health Services Administration, 2022). Globally, the prevalence of the so-called life style diseases such as heart disease, stroke, depression, diabetes, and obesity is becoming a major public health issue. Recent studies suggest that daily contact with nature has a long-lasting and deep impact on health—including depression and anxiety symptoms, birth weight, diabetes, obesity, heart disease, and longevity. It is therefore increasingly recognized that regular contact with nature is a major health determinant, and promoting interactions with nature may be a powerful, inexpensive form of preventive medicine.

By promoting a reconnection with nature and encouraging clients to spend intentional time in the natural world, ecotherapists foster the experience of reconnecting with our evolutionary home. When we prescribe time in nature, we are encouraging *interacting* with the natural world, developing a reciprocal relationship with it, and reconnecting with a deep knowing that is within each of us. Ecotherapists invite clients to slow the pace of life and be open to hearing their own internal voice. We encourage a respite from technology and a rebalancing of attention.

Ecotherapy invites experiences into the therapeutic process that afford an opportunity for thoughts, feelings, and ideas to become more deeply embodied; they fuel concern and affiliation, thus caring, for the natural world. An ecotherapist may write nature prescriptions that encourage clients to come to know a special place intimately, fostering a gradual deepening of connection, heightened sensory perception, and expanded knowledge of the place and a sense of belonging. They may encourage clients to spend time alone in a natural setting such as walking in the woods, sitting by a lake or river, or walking the water's edge at the beach while noticing the nature around them. Ecotherapists may ask clients to journal about an issue of concern during a natural transition time such as a sunrise or sunset, to plant a garden or window box, or to become involved in a community restoration project. These experiences foster a sense of nature connectedness. Research shows that the quality of our relationship with nature contributes to its impact on our health and well-being. Not surprisingly, people with strong nature connectedness are more likely to engage in more pro-environmental behaviors. Human health and planetary health are connected and must be considered in treating our mental health and physical well-being.

The practice of ecotherapy is well positioned to address the chronic psychological impacts of climate change on an intimate level. The American Psychiatric Association defines ecoanxiety as "a chronic fear of environmental doom." Britain's prestigious medical journal, *The Lancet*, reports that symptoms associated with climate anxiety include panic attacks, insomnia, and obsessive thinking, potentially leading to increases in stress-related problems (Costello et al., 2009). A report by Clayton, Manning, et al. (2021) and issued by the American Psychological Association, Climate for Health, and ecoAmerica projected long-term societal damage caused by ecoanxiety including interpersonal and intergroup aggression and loss of social identity and cohesion, especially for Indigenous communities and those dependent on the natural environment.

Broadening the scope of treatment to include a client's relationship with the natural world allows climate-related trauma and ecoanxiety to be salient topics to address in therapy. Recent studies point to the deep concern, fear, and sense of hopelessness that many people feel on this topic. A 2021 study of 10,000 young people 16–25 years old in ten countries found that respondents across all countries were worried about climate change; 59% were very or extremely worried and 84% were at least moderately worried. More than half of the respondents reported feeling sad, anxious, angry, powerless, helpless, and guilty, and 75% said that they think the future is frightening (Hickman et al., 2021). If we do not include the human–nature relationship within our scope of treatment, we risk missing the source of these powerful emotions, and we may not even ask the appropriate questions to invite these topics into the therapeutic discussion. A broader scope allows therapists to ask different questions and consider deeper origins for the depression or anxiety issues that clients bring into the office. Drawing on the research we have available today, clinicians can incorporate nature-based methods to address these issues. Though not a panacea for all the issues that walk into the office, ecotherapy is a valuable tool to stand alongside other methods used in a clinical practice today.

HOW THIS BOOK IS ORGANIZED

This book is organized into three sections: Overview, The Practice of Ecotherapy, and Practical Considerations. Overview begins with this introductory chapter that defines ecotherapy, looks at how nature has been a part of the healing process since ancient times, and focuses on the relevance of ecotherapy in the clinical office today. Drawing on current research, it makes the case that prescribing nature interaction and incorporating other ecotherapeutic methods is a best practice for care. The Overview section includes chapters that address the theoretical foundations of ecotherapy practice, discuss the importance of expanding the context of care to include the ecological system we all live in, and review the current research on the restorative benefits of nature contact. Practical issues like assessing the clinical office space for its restorative qualities and the restorative effects of technological nature are considered.

The Practice of Ecotherapy section is the heart of the book. It begins with coverage of topics that examine the development of an environmental identity and the concept of the ecological Self. This section includes specific practices for incorporating nature-based methods in the office setting, as well as moving therapy outdoors. Another chapter focuses on the growing practice of writing nature prescriptions to extend the therapeutic process beyond the session. This section concludes with a chapter on how to incorporate the concept of therapeutic nature language, cocreated rituals, and nature-based metaphors into clinical practice.

The Practical Considerations section of the book opens with a chapter that looks at the challenges and ethical considerations that are unique to ecotherapy. Another chapter offers an overview of the various forms of ecotherapy such as horticulture therapy, animal-assisted therapy, and wilderness therapy and discusses ecotherapy's applicability for treatment offered to special populations. A chapter discusses how the individual therapist can address the impacts of climate change—acute trauma from weather-related disasters and the chronic stressors and powerful emotions in response to the gradual effects of climate change that often are not articulated by our clients. The chapter explores what promotes climate resilience and encourages preparedness. The final chapter summarizes how ecotherapy broadens and deepens the clinical work of the therapist, makes the connection between human health and planetary health, and suggests future directions for research, training, and practice.

DISCLAIMER FOR PRACTITIONERS

This book is not a substitute for professional training. As noted in a later chapter where ethical considerations of the practice of ecotherapy are discussed, professionals have an obligation to practice only within the boundaries of their training and competencies. As practitioners, we increase our liability when we move therapy outdoors. Though I hope the reader will be inspired to incorporate some of the activities and suggestions in this book, I caution you to take responsibility for the emotional and physical safety of your clients, so that professional codes and standards are not compromised.

2

THEORETICAL FOUNDATIONS OF ECOTHERAPY

With a growing interest in the nature-based methods of ecotherapy, it is important to define the grounding principles and theories that provide the foundation for the practice. Ecotherapy draws on a theory of a human–nature relationship, broadly termed *ecopsychology*. This chapter will begin with an overview of the historical context of ecopsychology and discuss its relevance today. I'll highlight the basic principles of ecopsychology and the five tenets of the field that are particularly salient for the practice of ecotherapy. Because ecotherapy is especially useful in addressing stress and related psychological issues such as depression and anxiety, we'll explore how stress reduction theory (SRT) supports the practice of ecotherapy. We'll also introduce attention restoration theory (ART), which has emerged as an important theory for understanding how the demands from the urban environment deplete our voluntary attention. Finally, we'll close the chapter by looking at how ecopsychological theory interfaces with other theoretical orientations that the clinician might be utilizing.

ECOPSYCHOLOGY

Ecopsychology is the psychological field of inquiry that focuses on humans' relationship with the natural world and looks at how we might integrate that relationship into our modern scientific, technological culture. In my earlier book, *Ecopsychology: Science, Totems, and the Technological Species,* my coauthor and I identified the part of us that needs that kinship with nature as our *totemic self.* We suggested that one of the greatest challenges of our modern time is to value and embrace our totemic self and integrate it into our scientific culture and with our technological selves (Kahn & Hasbach, 2012). Ecopsychology helps to generate the formal structure, language, theory, and future for this integration. Ecopsychology also has an important role to play in advancing research about the psychological impacts of climate change, as well as furthering the research on the many benefits of nature connection in our lives. A central assumption of ecopsychology is that our inner world and the outer world are intimately connected.

Brief Historical Overview of Ecopsychology

The origins of ecopsychology began in the 1960s as part of the counterculture movement that, among many other cultural transitions and advances, gave birth to the modern environmental movement. That movement challenged our worldview of nature at the time— stating that nature was not a mechanistic entity but a system that was alive, aware, and engaged in reciprocal interactions. Early theorists like Paul Shepard (1998) reminded us that humans came of age with daily contact and connection to abundantly diverse and wild nature. He posited that we need that diversity and wildness to flourish as a species. Foundational ideas and early innovations of the field grew alongside the environmental movement and the associated activism of the peace movement, the environmental justice movement, and the growing interest in various forms of nature-based spirituality (Berry, 1988), ecofeminism (Fox, 1995), environmental literacy (Orr, 1991), and deep ecology (Naess, 1995).

By the early 1990s, these ideas began to come together in a body of work called *ecopsychology,* a term coined by Theodore Roszak (1992) in his book *The Voice of the Earth: An Exploration of Ecopsychology.* This book introduced a new perspective in psychotherapy that defined sanity as having an awareness of the connection between the environment and the human soul. In it, Roszak sought to build a bridge between psychology and ecology, and he saw that connection as a path to address the growing ecological crisis. Roszak later coedited with Mary Gomes and Allan Kanner a volume entitled *Ecopsychology: Restoring the Earth, Healing the Mind* (1995) that brought together many of the early thinkers of the field and laid the groundwork for the various directions this new field would follow. The varied and broad reach ecopsychology aspired to is evident in the closing paragraph of the book's foreword by Lester Brown: "Ecopsychology brings together the sensitivity of therapists, the expertise of ecologists, and the ethical energy of environmental activists. Out of this rich mixture may arise a new, more effective, more philosophically grounded form of environmental politics" (p. xvi).

Like many emerging disciplines, ecopsychology struggled to find its place and purpose in the early days. One of the relevant issues for clinicians to understand is how the terms ecopsychology and ecotherapy were often conflated. I think it is important to make the distinction between the theory of ecopsychology and the practice of ecotherapy. Mental health clinicians generally have a strong foundation in several clinical theories such as cognitive–behavioral theory, psychoanalytic theory, family systems theory, and so on. Their work is grounded in their chosen theories, and their methods and practices grow out of those foundational theories. For our purposes, it is important to be clear that ecopsychology provides the foundational theory that supports the practices and methods of ecotherapy. While we clarify the distinction between ecopsychology and ecotherapy, it is important to recognize that the dialectic between the two further enriches the development of both.

Two additional psychological fields of inquiry are closely related to ecopsychology. While ecopsychology focuses on human relationships with the natural world through ecological and psychological perspectives, environmental psychology is concerned with how various environments including the natural environment, built environments, learning environments, and informational environments impact humans. Conservation psychology is concerned with how human behaviors impact the natural world and draws on social psychology to identify how messaging can effectively encourage proenvironmental behaviors. These three intersecting areas of inquiry (as illustrated below) all contribute to the practices and methods employed by ecotherapists, and they are at the heart of the Division 34 Society for Environmental, Population, and Conservation Psychology of the American Psychological Association, which can serve as a good resource for practitioners.

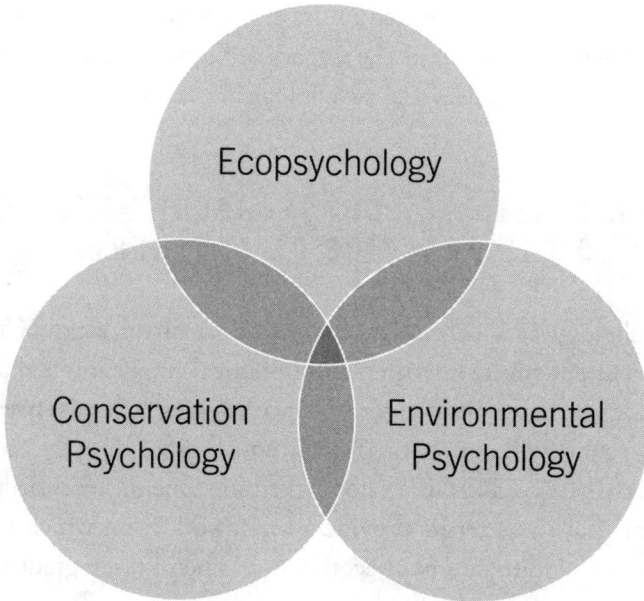

Figure 2.1 Related Psychology Fields

Why Ecopsychology Is More Relevant Than Ever

The theorical foundation of ecopsychology has much to offer clinicians as we wrestle with current topics such as:

- Humans' unprecedented distance from the natural world and the associated psychological and physical costs
- Increased presence of digital technology in our daily lives and the impact on humans' time and relationship with each other and with nature

- Climate change impacts contributing to chronic anxiety sometimes called ecoanxiety
- Emotional impacts of climate-related weather events such as hurricanes, tornadoes, wildfires, flooding, and drought
- Postpandemic awareness of our global interconnections and a growing awareness of the connection of human health and planetary health
- Social justice issues related to the environment
- A growing awareness of the impact of human–nature interactions on our physical and psychological health

FIVE TENETS OF ECOPSYCHOLOGY RELATED TO THE PRACTICE OF ECOTHERAPY

Ecopsychology as a field of inquiry covers a broad array of topics. Other volumes cover the societal and political implications that ecopsychology brings to bear on social concerns. Here I discuss five tenets of ecopsychology that provide the conceptual grounding for the practice of ecotherapy. This list is not etched in stone or necessarily even complete, but these tenets provide a framework from which to view the theoretical foundations of ecotherapy. When I teach graduate students, these tenets are highlighted:

1. Humans are biological beings with an evolutionary history, and many patterns of thought and action that formed through our co-evolving with nature are still with us.
2. Interactions with nature benefit people physically and psychologically.
3. Each individual is anchored within a larger universal identity related to our evolutionary origins that connects us to the living system of the Earth.
4. To flourish as individuals and as a species, we need to connect with wildness in the natural world and with the wildness that resides within each of us.

5. The ultimate source of meaning and value is found in the lived experience. For ecotherapy, the lived experience refers to direct sensorial contact with the natural world.

Biophilia and Evolutionary Psychology

The first tenet of ecopsychology that grounds the practice of eco-therapy focuses on the reality that we are biological beings with an evolutionary history, and many patterns of thoughts and action that formed through our co-evolving with nature are still with us. Our connection to nature is built in. Early 1900s medical dictionaries defined "biophilia" as the human instinct to stay alive. The biophilia hypothesis was proposed by the renowned Harvard biologist, E. O. Wilson (1984), to refer to what he and colleagues hypothesized as a fundamental, genetically based, and thus innate human tendency to affiliate with life. He sought to provide some understanding of how the human tendency to relate to life might be an expression of a biological need—one that is integral to human development. Wilson (1993) discussed how biophilia could have evolved through the lens of biocultural evolution. Genes that lead to behaviors that enhance survival tend to reproduce themselves, since they are carried in bodies that procreate more rather than less. In turn, those genes and correlative behaviors grow more frequent.

Studies on people's landscape preferences may offer similar insights to the impact of our evolutionary past. Human history probably began on the African savanna, a region with open grasslands, scattered trees, and denser greenery near water. Wilson (1984) noted that whenever people are given a choice of habitat, they move to open, tree-studded land on prominences overlooking water. It is not surprising that real estate prices are higher when they afford views, often from hilltops, because in our earlier evolutionary periods such spots increased safety and thus our chance for survival. Water views are especially prized; water is necessary for life.

A related study by Balling and Falk (1982) asked children of various ages living in the eastern United States for their preference ratings of five different biomes: rainforest, hardwood forest, boreal forest, savanna, and desert. They hypothesized that since Homo sapiens came of age on the savannas of East Africa, the younger children would prefer the savanna to the other biomes. Since familiarity with an environment was also believed to be a factor in environmental preference and since increasing age would correspond to the children's increasing familiarity with their own environments (hardwood forest), the researchers also hypothesized that the older children would equally prefer the hardwood forest and savanna and would prefer both over the other three biomes. The results from their study supported both hypotheses.

Other studies have shown individual preference for natural landscapes over built ones and built environments with water, trees, and vegetation over built ones without these features. Today, biophilic design is incorporated into health care facilities, hospitals, schools and other learning centers and into community and city planning.

Another interesting example of a possible behavioral link to our evolutionary history involves the practice of sending flowers. According to the theory of biophilia, we send flowers to people who are sick or in mourning, or who are celebrating an event, because flowers carry deep meaning within us. We are drawn to flowers because they were highly valued by our early ancestors as indicators of food and possible sources of water.

Similarly, a 2022 report by the National Oceanic and Atmospheric Administration (NOAA) estimated that 45 million people in the United States engage in bird watching as a hobby. The enjoyment of this activity may be a remnant from an earlier time when our survival depended on detailed and accurate identification of the natural world around us.

Biophilia has grown beyond a hypothesis, with robust empirical support over the last three decades demonstrating the quantifiable effects of interactions with nature on our mental health, physical health, and sense of well-being. Studies have shown that even minimal connections to nature such as looking out a window at green space increases productivity and job satisfaction in the workplace, promotes faster healing of patients in hospitals, and reduces the frequency of sickness in prisons. Creativity and imagination as well as emotional well-being have been shown to be the outcomes of interacting with nature.

As clinicians, we might think about what opportunities for human–nature interactions our healing spaces can offer. We might ask what happens to our cognitive abilities, our emotions, and our mental health if we are no longer interacting with nature on a regular basis. This leads us to the second tenet of ecopsychology related to ecotherapy, that interaction with nature benefits people physically and psychologically.

Interaction With Nature Benefits People Physically and Psychologically

During the last several decades, research has provided a robust and expansive body of quantitative and qualitative evidence about the health benefits gained by interacting with nature. I'll begin by highlighting a few of the classic studies that clinicians should be aware of and on whose work subsequent research has been built.

In a classic study conducted by Roger Ulrich (1984) and published in the journal *Science,* he compared how a hospital room with a view of deciduous trees versus a room with a view of a brick wall affected the recovery of patients after gall bladder surgery. Patients were assigned randomly to one or the other kind of room. The records of all cholecystectomy patients over a 10-year period, restricted to the summer months when the trees were in foliage, were reviewed. Compared to patients with the brick wall view, patients with the trees view had shorter postoperative hospital stays, had fewer negative evaluative comments from nurses, needed less pain medication, and had lower scores for minor postsurgical complications.

Moore (1981) studied the effects of views of landscapes on prison inmates in a Michigan prison. Half of the inmates occupied cells along the outside wall of the prison with a window view of farmland and trees, while the other half of the inmates occupied cells that faced the prison yard. Assignment to the cells were random. Compared to the inmates with the exterior cells with the outdoor view, the inmates with the inside cells had a 24% higher frequency of sick call visits.

In a study conducted in a dental office waiting room, researchers placed a large mural of an open, natural scene on the wall on some days and removed it on others. Dental patients with appointments on the days the mural was present reported less anxiety and had lower blood pressure than the patients with appointments on the days the mural was not present (Heerwagen, 1990).

Several studies provide empirical evidence of mental health benefits of contact with plants. In several studies of patients recovering from surgery, those who had plants in their hospital rooms reported less pain, less need for pain medication, less anxiety and fatigue, and higher satisfaction with their hospital stay, and they had lower systolic blood pressure and heart rates compared to patients without plants in their room (Park & Mattson, 2009). Other studies have demonstrated that the presence of plants has a positive influence on office workers; they reported greater job satisfaction, had higher productivity, and had fewer sick days.

Another body of evidence comes from the literature on human–animal interaction. Beck and Katcher (1996) examined the influence of pets on the course of heart disease in 92 cardiac patients. Accounting for social variables known to be associated with mortality from heart disease, it was found that the mortality rate among people with pets was about one-third of patients without pets. There are hundreds of clinical reports that show when animals enter the lives of patients with Alzheimer's disease, the patients smile and laugh more and become less hostile to caretakers and more socially communicative. Beck and Meyers (1996) reported that 50% of adults and 70% of adolescents confide in their animals. There is an expansive body of evidence that links our relationship to animals with human health. Think about the implications of this evidence for therapy. In Chapter 9, we explore various animal-assisted therapies.

Bratman and colleagues (2015) reported on the impact of nature experience on affect and cognition. The researchers randomly assigned 60 participants to a 50-minute walk in either a natural or urban environment in and around the Stanford University campus. Participants completed a series of psychological assessments of affective and cognitive functioning. Compared to the urban walkers, the nature walk resulted in affective benefits (e.g., decreased anxiety, rumination, and negative affect) and preserved positive affect as well as offered cognitive benefits in increased working memory performance.

Zelenski and Nisbet (2014) found that there is a unique connection between nature connectedness and happiness. Their research suggests that our emotional connection to the natural world is distinct from other psychological connections in our lives and that nature relatedness often predicts happiness regardless of other psychological factors.

This is just a sampling of the empirical evidence that exists in support of the tenet that interaction between humans and nature is beneficial for human health and well-being. I will cite additional research throughout the book as it relates to the topics discussed in the following chapters.

At no time in history has there been so much interest in the connection of nature and health as there is now, since the COVID-19 pandemic. We can leverage that interest in our practice as behavioral health providers.

Ecological Unconscious and Deep Ecology

Another tenet of ecopsychology that is important for ecotherapy states that individuals are anchored within a larger universal identity that is related to our evolutionary origins and connects us to the living system of the Earth. This tenet draws on the concept of the ecological unconscious and the philosophical grounding of deep ecology. Roszak (1992) introduced the concept of the ecological unconscious, likening it to Jung's concept of the collective unconscious. Roszak discusses how Jung originally conceptualized the collective unconscious as a repository for the compounded evolutionary history of our species. He quotes Jung, "Just as the body has its evolutionary history and shows clear traces of the various evolutionary states, so too does the psyche" (p. 302). According to Jungians, humans inherit the collective unconscious as primordial images that include all of our human ancestors as well as our prehuman or animal ancestors. The deepest substratum of the collective unconscious is our archaic prehuman experience (Roszak, 1992). For Roszak, this deep level of the collective unconscious held the essence of the ecological unconscious. Jung later modified his conception of the collective unconscious to make it more exclusively human and focused it more on the cultural realm and connected to the great religious symbols of humanity.

Roszak conceptualized the ecological unconscious as the repository of an evolutionary record that ties the psyche to the universe's full cosmic history. He referred to Gaia theory and deep ecology, which posits that the Earth is a living system of which we humans are a part. Each individual is anchored within a larger universal identity related to our evolutionary origins. Through this lens, we each have the potential for deep and meaningful connection to the more-than-human world.

In the epilogue of *The Voice of the Earth*, Roszak calls on therapists to listen to the whole person including all that is submerged beneath culture. He provides a list of principles that are intended to be a guide for how deep that listening must go to hear "the Self speak through the self" (p. 320). Like much of the early writings in ecopsychology, the work of therapists and the work of social activists are conflated in Roszak's principles. For the clinician reading this book, I summarize a few of these principles that relate specifically to therapy and add ideas of how the principle may be applied in practice. But for a full understanding of Roszak's conceptualization of ecopsychology, I urge the reader to look at his book, *The Voice of the Earth*.

1. The ecological unconscious concept reminds us that unconscious processes exist within us. Practitioners are mostly schooled in these intrapsychic processes as they relate to other people—especially our initial caregivers and our partners. The ecological unconscious extends our intrapsychic processes to the earth itself, specifically, the processes of identification and repression. According to Roszak, repression of the ecological unconscious is the deepest root of our environmental crisis, and open access to the ecological unconscious is the path to sanity.

2. The content of the ecological unconscious represents the living record of cosmic evolution—the unfolding of physical, biological, psychological, and cultural systems that form the universe. Ecotherapy can incorporate this cosmological access through nature imagery and therapeutic metaphor and through direct experience with the natural world.

3. Traditional therapy seeks to heal the alienation between individuals, between the individual and their family, and between the individual and society. Ecopsychology seeks to heal the alienation between the person and the natural world and awaken the inherent sense of environmental reciprocity that lies within the ecological unconscious.

4. The ecological unconscious is regenerated in each child's enchanted view of the world. Ecopsychology seeks to preserve the child's innately animistic quality of experience and reintroduce that experience of enchantment with the natural world.

5. Through identification within the ecological unconscious, humans recognize their ethical responsibility to the planet as clearly as we experience our ethical responsibility to other people. Ecopsychology recognizes that human health and planetary health are interdependent.

As we contemplate the content of the ecological unconscious as the living record of our evolutionary journey, we begin to realize that we need to experience the complexity, the beauty, and the awesome power of the natural world to flourish as individuals and as a species. When we allow ourselves to take that in, most of us experience some sense of awe and humility. Difficulty in accessing this sense of awe and humility stems from our hearts and minds being closed because of our cultural emphasis on autonomy, separation, convenience, speed, and efficiency. This leads us to the fourth tenet of ecopsychology that relates to ecotherapy: To flourish as individuals and as a species, we need to connect with wildness in the natural world and wildness within ourselves. This is sometimes referred to as human rewilding.

Human Rewilding

To flourish as individuals and as a species, we need to connect more deeply with wildness in the natural world and with the wildness that resides in each of us. As I have written elsewhere (Kahn & Hasbach, 2012, 2013), wildness in the natural world often involves that which is big, untamed, unmanaged, self-organizing, and unencumbered by technology and human intervention. We can love the wild. We can fear it. But we are strengthened and nurtured by it. Our Paleolithic ancestors lived a life far wilder than we do today, and much of that wildness still exists within the architecture of our bodies and minds. But so much of our contemporary experience of the environment around us is filtered through human-made technologies—from the heated and cooled air in our buildings, to electric lights that burn into the night, to filtered and conditioned water that comes from the tap, to enclosed vehicles that shuttle us about at high speed, to the ever-present screens that seduce our attention and offer a two-dimensional view of the world. To flourish as a species, that wildness needs to be rediscovered, reengaged, and reintegrated into our lives.

But how does human rewilding impact the practice of ecotherapy? Earlier I discussed how our time and attention are heavily weighted to indoor living and focused on the digital technology we've created. Human rewilding reminds us of our out-of-balance state, and offers a path to intentionally reconnect ourselves to the more-than-human world. The wild side of human nature is often thought to be at odds with civilization. We'll see in later chapters how important acknowledgment of the primal Self is to well-being, to a feeling of belonging to something bigger than ourselves, to experiencing awe and humility, and to feeling fully alive. Human rewilding will play a part in incorporating therapeutic nature language into the prescriptions written by the ecotherapist, and it will be essential in listening for and utilizing nature metaphors and imagery in the therapeutic dialogue. Human rewilding is also useful as we encourage heightened sensorial awareness and direct experiences in nature. This leads us to our final tenet of ecopsychology that relates to ecotherapy: The ultimate source of meaning and value is the lived experience. For ecotherapy, this involves direct sensorial interactions with the natural world.

Phenomenology

Phenomenology is grounded in European philosophers such as Edmund Husserl and Maurice Merleau-Ponty, who believed that direct experience is the source of knowledge. Phenomenology is the study of phenomena—how we experience things and the meaning we assign to them—from a first-person point of view. For phenomenology, the ultimate source of meaning and value is the lived experience. For ecotherapy, that lived experience refers to direct sensorial contact with the phenomena of nature. For some people, this direct experience and associated meaning derived from it can be contextualized as a spiritual experience. Though scientists are reluctant to acknowledge such experiences because they have traditionally been conceptualized in supernatural terms, it is possible to conceptualize spiritual phenomena in psychological terms that do not require belief in supernatural entities. As Maslow (1974) pointed out, when spiritual phenomena are recognized as being psychological in nature, they become a legitimate topic for scientific discussion. In a spiritual experience, a person encounters something greater than one's individual self. In some important way the experience gives meaning to one's life and helps to define who one is in relation to the world or the universe. The experience is felt at a level deeper than the intellectual, and it is more than an abstract thought. It may be difficult to express in words, but it is felt in the body and may produce powerful emotions. Schroeder (2012) used open-ended surveys about people's special outdoor places to show that aesthetic and other kinds of positive experiences in these places were much more than a pleasant amenity. These special places served as a source of meaning and happiness and led people to form emotional attachments to the place. He stated, "The experiential value of an environment may be strongly present in a person's awareness and may be an important facet of their quality of life, but they may have trouble finding words to convey that value" (p. 137). Schroeder draws on the experiential psychologist Eugene Gendlin and others to illustrate how an initially inarticulate, body-felt sense of experiential value of a natural environment can be explained in a way that articulates the implicit value experienced and leads to a sense of well-being and nature connectedness. This body-felt experience is often described as a deep sense of belonging, connectedness to place or Other, or the experience of awe.

For the ecotherapist, the direct experiences the client has with the natural world and the meaning they assign to it is at the heart of the therapeutic work. We will explore how this *felt sense* may impact one's environmental identity in Chapter 5, and we'll highlight the importance of encouraging a felt sense of nature connectedness into nature prescriptions and outdoor work with clients in the Practice section of this book.

As ecotherapists, we might ask: What happens when one ceases to have direct experiences in the natural world? How does this extinction of experience affect the individual? Since research suggests that to truly care about the natural world, one must experience meaningful interaction with it, what influence does a diminished experience of nature have on conservation efforts and on the recognition of the connection between human health and planetary health?

STRESS REDUCTION THEORY AND ATTENTION RESTORATION THEORY

There are two major theories that help to explain the restorative power of nature interaction, and they provide foundational support for many ecotherapy activities. Each of these theories will be elaborated on in Chapter 4, but here I offer a brief overview. Both have their roots in evolutionary theory. The evolutionary perspective holds that because humans came of age over a long period of time in natural environments, people are physiologically and psychologically better adapted to natural environments than to urban environments. Stress reduction theory (SRT) emphasizes the role of nature contact on affect and in relieving physiological stress, whereas attention restoration theory (ART) focuses on the role of nature in relieving mental stress and attention fatigue.

Stress Reduction Theory

Stress reduction theory provides an explanation for the restorative impact of nature experience after a stressful situation. When faced with an unexpected stressor, the sympathetic branch of the autonomic nervous system goes into action, preparing the body to respond. This response is often referred to as the *fight-or-flight* response. The parasympathetic branch of the autonomic nervous system is responsible for recuperating from a stressful stimulus and returning the body to a state of equilibrium. According to stress reduction theory, natural scenes activate the parasympathetic nervous system in ways that reduce stress and autonomic arousal because of our innate connection to the natural world. Thus, affective reactions to environments may happen at a preconscious level and may impact cognitive processes without an individual's conscious knowledge. In other words, just viewing nature or being in the presence of nearby nature can reduce stress through automatic psychological and physiological responses.

Attention Restoration Theory

Attention restoration theory posits that humans utilize two types of attention: voluntary attention that is required to concentrate on work involving detail such as hours spent in front of a computer screen or poring over spreadsheets and involuntary attention that happens when we are free to notice what is naturally fascinating to us. Stephen and Rachel Kaplan formulated a theory that examines the ways in which exposure to nature can have a restorative effect on the brain's ability to focus and recover. The theory posits that directed attention requires the use of cognitive control to focus on a stimulus that may or may not have attracted one's attention. To do this, an individual must suppress the urge to be distracted (Kaplan, 1995). This capacity to concentrate can become fatigued and lead to difficulties in concentration and to irritability. By contrast, involuntary attention happens when individuals are presented with stimuli that are "inherently intriguing" (p. 171). ART suggests that interacting with nature through viewing natural scenes or taking in natural stimuli sensorially rests our directed attention and allows for its restoration. The specific components of attention restoration theory are discussed in detail in Chapter 4. As ecotherapists, we might ask what happens with stress recovery when humans are removed from regular contact with nature, and how might we incorporate natural stimuli into our healing environments to facilitate the therapeutic process.

THE INTERFACE BETWEEN
ECOPSYCHOLOGY THEORY AND OTHER
THEORETICAL ORIENTATIONS

Ecopsychology theory is compatible with many of the theoretical orientations employed by practicing psychotherapists. Here are a few examples.

Gestalt theory emphasizes the importance of the here and now. Being fully present to an experience in the natural world by intentionally engaging all the senses is a central component of ecopsychology. Both theories draw on systems theory and they look at aspects of the human experience that are difficult to measure empirically.

Both Jungian theory and ecopsychology theory are concerned with the loss of nature connection. The concept of the ecological unconscious rests at the deepest level of the collective unconscious as it was originally envisioned by Jung. The *archaic man* of Jungian theory and the *primal self* of ecopsychology theory both refer to our original, authentic Self that is sought in the therapeutic process.

Transpersonal psychology focuses on the interface of psychology and spirituality with interests in optimizing mental health and psychological development. The concepts of peak experiences and nonduality, as well as the promotion of reciprocity, humility, and awe are shared by both transpersonal psychology theory and ecopsychology theory.

Positive psychology outlines the various components of well-being that include happiness, purpose, finding meaning in life, and fulfillment. Psychological well-being also includes resilience and the ability to problem-solve and sustain healthy relationships. A wealth of evidence links nature experience with increased positive affect, happiness, positive social interactions, a sense of meaning and purpose in life, and decreased mental distress.

Humanistic psychology focuses on the whole person approach and looks at the uniqueness of each individual. Humanistic psychology values phenomenology and looks at the individual in their environmental context. Ecopsychology theory values direct experiences and the meaning derived and looks at the individual from a holistic perspective that includes not only their intrapsychic influences, but also their interpersonal relationships, their family system, and their societal influences, and the ecological system in which they live. This holistic perspective will be explored further in Chapter 3.

As a clinician, what are the theoretical orientations that shape your work, and how do you see ecopsychology interfacing with those orientations?

3

EXPANDING THE
CONTEXT OF CARE

Historically, psychotherapy has focused on human-to-human relationships. Our understanding of the complexity of relationship is reflected in the development of psychology's 200-year history. We think of modern psychology (and psychotherapy) beginning with Sigmund Freud, Carl Jung, Alfred Adler, and their contemporaries in the early 1900s. Their writings and early theoretical development focused on the intrapsychic processes within the individual. Though many of these early theories have been updated or refuted, they laid the initial foundation for understanding the complexity of the human experience. These pioneers of the mind sought to explain human behavior, and they explored ideas of unconscious motivations, fantasies, spirituality, dreams, sexuality, and experiences of denial, regression, attachment, and trauma. These theorists and their followers were also interested in how intrapsychic phenomena influenced the individual's interpersonal relationships—especially the relationships with early caregivers and intimate partners.

In the 1950s, systems theory was introduced into psychotherapy. Systems theory is not a single theoretical approach, but rather an epistemological approach that includes a wide range of applications in various fields (Sexton & Stanton, 2016). Systems theory marked the shift away from intrapsychic analysis to a focus on how reciprocal influences between individuals in relationships occurred. The deep influence of the family of origin and the current family structure of the client began to be more fully appreciated and studied. Through the lens of systems theory, clinicians began to understand the individual within the context of the family system.

Out of systems theory grew a greater appreciation for the impact of societal norms and roles on the individual, as well as the deep influence of cultural worldviews. Systems theory broadens our clinical focus and considers how the larger outer world shapes the individual. The 1960s and 70s brought awareness of the power of cultural "isms"—racism, sexism, ageism, and so on—and their influence on each person. Societal influences such as workplace stress, educational environment, and health care access began to find their way into the therapy room.

But until the introduction of ecopsychology in the 1990s, most traditional psychology theory and psychotherapy practice stopped at the urban boundary. We did not look at the impact of the ecological system out of which the individual grew or in which they lived. Because much of the dominant Western culture saw humans as separate from nature, practitioners did not consider the individual's ecological experiences as a factor in their well-being. We did not recognize the potential therapeutic benefits of a reciprocal relationship between humans and the natural world. Similarly, global environmental concerns were not thought to impact the mental health of the individual. David Orr (2009) goes so far as to say that mental health therapy helped clients fit into an insane world rather than focus on healing the relationship between humans and nature.

Until recently, most practitioners did not view the client's ecological system to be connected to their well-being or their mental health. The relationship between the individual and the natural environment was not included in the clinician's training. The *Diagnostic and Statistical Manual*, used worldwide to diagnose mental health issues, does not mention any relationship to the environment, except noting seasonal influence on major depression disorder. Similarly, clients rarely voiced concerns for the environment in the context of therapy because they did not expect those concerns to be a focus of the therapeutic process. Without expanding our therapeutic lens to include the ecological system, clinicians risk missing the opportunity to fully grasp the client's

experience of nature and their concerns for it. If we treat what therapists call the presenting problem only within the human-to-human
context, we may fail to acknowledge deeper existential issues. If we
don't ask about such concerns, we may contribute to the client's feelings of despair, loneliness, and alienation. We may not consider the
deeper etiology of depression and/or anxiety, and we may overlook a
powerful healing partner in nature.

In the last decade, a wealth of studies has demonstrated that nature
experience is associated with psychological well-being. Evidence links
nature experience with increased positive affect, happiness and subjective well-being, positive social interactions and community cohesion, and a sense of meaning and purpose in life. Longitudinal studies
and controlled experiments have shown nature experience to positively affect cognitive function, memory, and attention; improve children's school performance; and enhance imagination and creativity
(Bratman et al., 2019).

Today, with a definitive body of research that demonstrates the psychological importance of the ecological system in which the individual is embedded, ecopsychology draws on systems theory to include
the more-than-human world. By expanding the lens with which we
view the client and the various therapeutic contexts, clinicians open
new possibilities for deepening therapy.

Think about the therapeutic lens with which you, as a clinician,
view your clients. Typically, when meeting with a client, therapists
are concerned with: the intrapsychic processes at work within the client; we consider the interpersonal relationships the client is involved
in; we ask about the client's family of origin and the existing family
system they are living with; and we look at the social and cultural
influences in their lives. We can imagine the client nested in all these
various contexts of their life. We can view these contexts of life like
the lens of a camera—each widening the scope of treatment focus.
During the treatment planning process, we consider the various focal
points where transformation is possible. Ecotherapy expands the
treatment focus further to recognize the ecological system in which
the client is a part. By expanding the scope of treatment to include
the human–nature relationship, we invite clients to acknowledge their

relationship with the natural world or their feelings of disconnection from it. Topics such as environmental concerns, climate-related trauma, and ecoanxiety become relevant topics for therapy. Clients can express their feelings of despair, fear, apathy, guilt, and helplessness, as well as feelings of joy, a sense of belonging, groundedness, and strength. Figure 3.1 illustrates an expanded context of care where the individual is embedded in all these contexts.

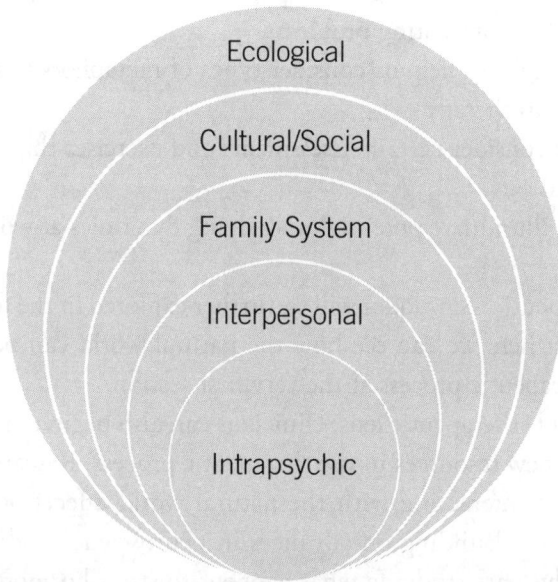

Figure 3.1 Contexts of Care

As the clinician's lens broadens their view of the client, new questions emerge. During the intake session, the client might be asked about a childhood memory they have of time spent interacting with nature. We might ask about how their family of origin viewed the natural world. To better understand how the client experiences nature now, we might ask what they like to do outdoors and how often they do it. Answers to these questions provide initial information about the client's historical and current relationship with nature. By incorporating these types of questions into the intake session, we acknowledge the client's relationship with the natural world and make that relationship an appropriate topic for therapy. The responses to these questions provide valuable information to the therapist to use in formulating a treatment plan and laying the groundwork for future discussions. Answers to these intake questions:

- Provide insight about whether the client might benefit from moving sessions outdoors
- Provide information regarding possible nature prescriptions to help address presenting problems
- Offer insight to help us consider types of metaphors to incorporate into therapy
- Help us consider certain assessments and exercises that might be useful
- Help to illuminate potential underlying dynamics at work

These therapeutic techniques will be further explored in the following chapters, but here we can see how the natural world can be invited into the therapeutic process at the very first session.

With a wide therapeutic lens, clinicians can also begin to recognize and employ new resources in the therapeutic process. Researchers are studying how interacting with the natural world affects our brains and our bodies. Building on advances in neuroscience and psychology, researchers are studying what happens to stress hormones, heart rates, and brain waves when we spend time in green and blue spaces.

David Strayer, a professor and researcher specializing in attention at the University of Utah, has been studying the effect of long-term exposure to green space. In an interview with Florence Williams (2016) for *National Geographic*, Strayer says, "There is something profound going on" as he studies what is now called the *three-day effect*. The three-day effect refers to the results of studies that found participants experienced a kind of neural reboot after being out in nature, removed from the stress of their daily life and digital technology. Their cognitive performance increased, their mood improved, and their creativity was heightened. Strayer has also conducted several studies to investigate the effects of being in nature on participants' working memory and attention restoration. His studies have shown that when we are fully present, not distracted by our technology (e.g., cell phones), it produces a difference in qualitative thinking (Atchley et al., 2012). His findings are consistent with the Kaplans' attention restoration theory that we will read more about in the next chapter.

Many of the nature-based practices and methods of ecotherapy invite a reconnection with wild nature and the wilder ecological Self. Ecotherapy recognizes that a part of our deep knowing can be accessed if we are willing to move outdoors and experience nature fully and mindfully. Ecotherapists invite clients to take the therapeutic work into nature through assigning nature prescriptions for clients to do between sessions and/or by moving the therapy sessions outdoors. Direct experience in nature affords heightened sensorial experiences and perceptions that connect our inner world with the outer landscape. Through an increased consciousness of their ecological community, clients can widen their circle of identification and become more aware of their sense of place and feelings of kinship and belonging to something bigger than themselves. Ecotherapists invite clients to slow their pace of life, move outdoors, notice what draws their attention, and be open to hearing their own internal voice. We encourage a respite from technology and invite a rebalancing of attention (Hasbach, 2015).

In my practice, I regularly prescribe nature time to clients that takes them outdoors between our scheduled sessions. I may ask a client to visit a favorite *sit spot* several times each week for a month and form a relationship with that place. Over the course of a month or so, this exercise fosters a gradual deepening of connection, a heightened sensory perception, an expanded knowledge of the place, and a sense of familiarity or belonging. Experiences like this one also provide rich images and metaphors to work with during subsequent therapy sessions.

Adding the ecological system to our scope of treatment focus provides a more holistic view of the individual's experience in the world and their relationship with nature. As issues related to our rapidly changing environment show up in the nightly news, and as more people are directly impacted by increasingly frequent and intense climate-related weather events, more clients are presenting with climate-related concerns and acute trauma. In the following chapters, we will look at how the client's ecological system might be an integral part of their identity and provide a source of strength and support as they navigate difficult life events. We will also see how making the human–nature relationship an appropriate topic for therapy invites concerns about the future. We'll explore how couples' issues related to the environment and their views about the world impact couples therapy. We'll explore how some young people are forgoing advanced education because of the despair they feel about the future and discuss how we might foster hope by looking to nature. We'll look at *psychoterractic conditions*—a new term used to describe a set of emotions related to the changing environment that Glenn Albrecht (2012), an Australian professor of environmental studies coined. We'll discover how the concept of therapeutic nature language can provide a systematic way to identify human–nature interactions and how that concept might be employed in therapy. Expanding our clinical lens to include the natural environment in which we are all embedded opens profound topics and rich resources for the therapeutic process.

4

RESTORATIVE BENEFITS OF NATURE INTERACTION

A few months ago, a client I was seeing for the fifth session came into my office, took her seat on the couch across from me, broke into a big smile and said, "I love being in this space!" When I asked what she found so appealing she mentioned the view of the tree canopy with the morning light filtering through the bright green leaves, the sound of the water from the table fountain, the fresh cut flowers next to me, the open, uncluttered room, and the calming color palette. I appreciated her comments. I put a lot of thought into the physical space where I meet with clients, and I have been intentional about incorporating elements of nature into the therapeutic space. Physical settings can play an important role in fostering a sense of well-being, mitigating stress, and providing a safe and restorative atmosphere.

I imagine most clinicians strive to create an environment that feels inviting, warm, and physically and emotionally safe for clients. Ecotherapists also think about how to bring the natural world indoors, and we are mindful of the outdoor spaces where we meet clients. It's important that we consider what the science tells us about what makes a place healing and restorative.

Acknowledging the role of nature experience in mental health has been part of the dialogue surrounding the human–nature relationship for a long time. In an article from the *Annals of the New York Academy of Science*, Bratman and his colleagues (2012) remind us that John Muir and the originators of the Wilderness Act in the United

States discussed nature's contribution to mental health specifically. The article also references the work by Marcus and Barnes (1999) on the history of healing gardens in hospital settings. Those authors trace the incorporation of healing gardens and natural areas in infirmaries back to the Middle Ages, referring to nearly thousand-year-old writings by St. Bernard that support the healing effects of these natural spaces. They follow what are called *courtyard traditions* in hospitals through the English, German, and French designs of hospitals of the 1600–1800s. Remnants of these traditions are still found in nature walks, herbal remedies, and mud baths in mainstream German health care (Bratman et al., 2012).

This chapter focuses on how we can incorporate nature into the design of our healing spaces and summarizes the current research on the therapeutic and restorative benefits of nature contact by viewing nature, being in the presence of nearby nature, and by active nature immersion. We will consider two theories that were introduced earlier in Chapter 2: stress reduction theory (SRT) and attention restoration theory (ART). Both complementary theories have their roots in evolutionary psychology and biophilia. Attention restoration theory addresses the *cognitive* impact of nature experiences while stress reduction theory provides an explanation for the impact of nature experience on *affect*. We'll explore the components of restorative environments in ART and identify environmental characteristics that promote restoration. We'll put this knowledge into practice by offering you the opportunity to assess your office space for its restorative qualities. The chapter concludes with a look at the restorative effects of vicarious nature and its applicability to therapeutic practice.

THE EVIDENCE FOR THE RESTORATIVE BENEFIT OF NATURE INTERACTION

Most contemporary studies on the restorative benefits of nature interaction use a comparative approach whereby the experience of individuals within one environment is contrasted with the experience of individuals within another environment, where one environment is more natural or includes more nature than the other. An example would be walking on a nature trail versus walking on an urban street. I've included studies here that attempted to document the psychological impacts of nature interaction in a scientifically rigorous way. These studies draw heavily on Kellert and Wilson's (1993) biophilia hypothesis that states that humans have a universal and innate need to affiliate with nature.

Wilson (1993) also emphasized our need to feel a sense of belonging to the natural world. Kellert (2012) points out that our inborn affinity for nature must be cultivated and nurtured through learned experience, sustained engagement, and with the support of others. This raises questions about what happens to our cognitive abilities, emotional states, and mental health—not to mention our interconnectedness and sense of reciprocity with nature—if we are increasingly removed from the natural world. With increased urbanization, a growing technological presence in our daily lives, an accelerated pace of life, and virtual experiences replacing real ones, we are interacting with nature far less than any time in our species' history. Not only do we have fewer opportunities to engage with nature, but based on the statistics from the National Human Activity Pattern Survey, people now spend nearly 90% of their time indoors (Yin et al., 2020).

Biophilic design is a relatively new approach that attempts to incorporate the positive experience of nature into the built environment by bringing nature into living and working spaces. In clinic settings, studies found that natural sounds, aromatherapy, green plants, and views of nature in hospital interior spaces reduced mental stress, increased pain tolerance, and shortened hospital stays. Research continues to better understand how different elements of biophilic design contribute to these health and well-being outcomes. Practitioners are taking notice and becoming more intentional about including natural elements into their varied healing spaces. Dental offices, physician's waiting rooms, hospital rooms, and clinics are adding natural elements and nature-based art. Ecotherapists include nature elements in their office space to stimulate the senses, to invite the outdoors in, and to incorporate the current research into their practice.

During the last two decades, a large body of research has offered evidence on the various health benefits of nature contact that includes: reduced stress, improved sleep, reduced depression, lessening of anxiety, greater happiness and sense of well-being, increased life satisfaction, reduced aggression, reduced ADHD symptoms, and increased prosocial behavior and pro-environmental behaviors (Frumkin et al., 2017). This research also examines the benefits of interactions with nature to cognitive capacities such as attention, memory, and impulse control.

This is not to imply that biophobia or negative psychological effects from nature experience are not possible as well. Fear of being in unfamiliar environments, concern about unpredictable wildlife, and anxiety about the impacts by natural disasters such as wildfires, hurricanes, or earthquakes bring their own levels of stress that are being increasingly addressed by researchers and practitioners—particularly as they relate to climate-related weather events. We'll look at that topic more fully in Chapter 10.

STRESS REDUCTION THEORY

According to stress reduction theory, natural scenes activate the parasympathetic nervous system in ways that reduce stress and autonomic arousal because of our innate connection to the natural world. According to Ulrich (1983), landscapes with views of water and/or vegetation and that have modest depth and complexity would have been most beneficial for our ancestors' survival. These landscapes help to moderate and diminish states of arousal and negative thoughts within minutes through psychophysiological pathways (Bratman et al., 2012). Thus, affective reactions to environments may happen at a preconscious level and may impact cognitive processes without an individual's conscious knowledge. Viewing these landscapes activates our physiology in ways beneficial to affect.

Ulrich put his hypothesis to the test in a series of studies. In one study, Ulrich and colleagues (1991) had 120 subjects watch a stressful movie for 10 minutes and then view scenes with sound of six different types of settings, ranging from most urban setting to most natural setting for another 10 minutes. Subjects were monitored for levels of physiological stress through measures of heart rate, skin conductance, muscle tension, and blood pressure. Study participants were also asked to self-rate their affect states. All measures indicated a significantly higher speed of recovery from stress when viewing nature scenes than when viewing urban scenes.

Other studies have added supporting evidence for SRT. Several studies on forest bathing in Japan have built on the classic work of Park and colleagues (2007). That study looked at the impact of forests versus urban landscapes on stress relief by transporting the study's subjects between forest and urban settings, while measuring cortisol levels in saliva, blood pressure, and pulse rate while the subjects were physically present in each setting. All the measures indicated significantly decreased stress for the subjects after being present in the forest setting for only 15 minutes—a result not found when they were in the urban setting.

Research such as these examples focuses on short-term indicators of stress recovery. Other research has focused on a longer time frame. Ward Thompson and colleagues (2016) compared people living in more and less green neighborhoods with regard to their subjective levels of stress or their ability to cope with stressful life events. The results consistently indicated that nature contact reduces stress and aids in stress recovery.

ATTENTION RESTORATION THEORY

Attention restoration theory emphasizes the role of nature in relieving mental fatigue and looks at ways in which interacting with nature can have a restorative effect on the brain's ability to focus. As summarized in Chapter 2, ART posits that humans utilize two types of attention: voluntary attention that requires the use of cognitive control to focus on a stimulus that may or may not hold our attention and requires us to suppress the urge to be distracted, thus leading to mental fatigue; and involuntary attention that we experience when the stimuli are "inherently intriguing" to us (Kaplan, 1995, p. 171). According to

ART, our interaction with natural environments utilizes our involuntary attention, thus allowing neural mechanisms underlying directed attention a chance to rest. The experience that comes from viewing nature or interacting with nature allows attentional reserves to replenish, which in turn can benefit performance on tasks that require concentration and perhaps even influence levels of depression and stress (Bratman et al., 2012).

Kaplan (1995) identified four essential components that are often found in natural environments that contribute to the restorative effects on our direct attention capacity:

1. *Being away:* involves removing ourselves from the stressors of daily life and/or from the work demanding our directed attention. How many of us have said "I'm looking forward to getting away to . . . the lake, the mountains, the beach . . . "? Being away can range from mini-escapes like taking a brief walk outdoors at lunchtime or shifting our focus from the computer screen to the bird feeders outside the window, to a daylong hike in the woods or paddle on the lake. Being away involves a conceptual transformation rather than a purely physical change, thus allowing our directed attention an opportunity to rest.

2. *Soft fascination:* refers to aspects of nature that innately hold our attention in an undramatic way, without directed effort. Examples include watching clouds move across the sky, enjoying the sun sinking below the horizon at sunset, and seeing the motion of leaves rustling in the wind. Soft fascination has the advantage of providing the opportunity for reflection, which can further enhance the benefits of recovery from directed attention fatigue.

3. *Extent:* refers to the scope of an experience like the vastness of a mountain landscape or the expansiveness of the ocean. Extent can also be experienced in smaller environments like a nearby park through the design of winding paths and trails that lead us to wonder what is around the next bend. Historical artifacts can promote a sense of connectedness to past eras. Extent leaves us feeling as if we are in a whole different world.

4. *Compatibility:* refers to a special resonance between the environment and human inclinations. A person would experience compatibility when their purpose or inclinations fits with the setting. Examples include a predator role one might experience when hunting or fishing, an observation role one might experience while bird watching, or a partnering with nature role experienced while gardening.

Natural environments most consistently include these four components identified as necessary for an environment to be restorative to our directed attention capacity. Through cognitive testing, researchers can measure whether replenishment has occurred after nature interaction. A few of these studies are discussed here.

Berman and colleagues (2008) used a backward digit span task (i.e., a test that measures working memory, thus measuring directed attention capacity) to test participants. The researchers then induced mental fatigue in the participants with a 35-minute test that taxed memory. Participants were randomly placed in two groups. One group walked through an urban setting, and the other group walked through an arboretum. Both walks were 2.8 miles and lasted approximately 50 minutes. Following the walk, participants performed the digit span backward task again. The group that walked in the arboretum performed significantly better on the memory/directed attention task than those who walked in the urban setting. The researchers also administered the Positive and Negative Affect Schedule (PANAS) questionnaire to participants and found an increase in positive affect in the arboretum walking group. Significant improvements in working memory were noted in a second study in which groups viewed pictures of nature versus pictures of urban settings.

To test the potential usefulness of natural images, Berto (2005) induced mental fatigue to study participants through the Sustained Attention to Response Test (SART), a 5-minute response-control test that requires subjects to press a button when a rarely occurring target digit appears on a computer screen, but not when other digits appear. The researcher then exposed participants to photos of natural scenes (i.e., restorative environments) or urban scenes (i.e., nonrestorative environments). Those who viewed natural photos performed significantly better on the second administration of the SART than those who had viewed urban images. Additionally, these results were consistent when subjects were exposed to natural scenes versus geometric figures, supporting the assertion of attention restoration theory that natural scenes have this type of restorative potential.

One field experimental study tested ART using mobile electroencephalography (EEG) to record and analyze the restorative experience of walkers in a green space setting (Roe et al., 2013). They found EEG signals were consistent with attentional restoration when participants were walking in the green space versus in an urban space.

Another study utilized mobile EEG to understand the impact of various urban environments (e.g., busy, quiet, and green urban spaces) on brain activity (Neale et al., 2020). Ninety-five older participants (over age 65) were assigned to one of six walks in an urban neighborhood, transitioning between two distinct environmental settings. This study explored changes in alpha (associated with relaxation) and beta (associated with attention) brain activity recorded during walking in differing urban environments. Neural activity significantly varied as participants walked between "urban busy" and urban green settings, with reduced levels of low beta activity in the green setting, suggesting attention changes consistent with attention restoration theory. Levels of alpha activity significantly varied between the urban busy and the "urban quiet" settings, with increases in the urban busy setting. There were no significant differences in EEG activity between the urban green and urban quiet settings, suggesting that the magnitude of environmental contrast between the urban busy context and other urban settings is an important factor in understanding the effects of these spaces on brain activity.

A robust body of research provides evidence that nature interaction—through viewing nature, interacting directly with nature, and looking at nature images—improves mental health and well-being through mechanisms that involve affect (i.e., one's mood) and stress reduction and by offering a reprieve to our directed attention. The next section explores how we can incorporate these research findings into our practice methods and our healing spaces.

CREATING A RESTORATIVE ENVIRONMENT

We have looked at examples of research that provides evidence demonstrating that spending time in nature-rich environments bolsters mental health, promotes a sense of well-being, and helps to reduce negative thoughts. This evidence has led an increasing number of health professionals to prescribe time in nature to their patients and incorporate nature elements into their healing spaces. For example, Nooshin Razani, a pediatrician at UCSF Benioff Children's Hospital in Oakland, California, writes prescriptions for children and their families to visit nearby parks and has added nature into the clinic space. Photos of local nature scenes line the walls, and maps of local parks are provided. Prescribing nature interactions falls under the umbrella of *social prescriptions* that include eating a diet rich in fruits and vegetables, exercising daily, getting adequate sleep, and so on. We will discuss nature prescriptions in Chapter 7.

In this section we look at how to put the research into practice as we consider the healing spaces where we work and meet with clients. To begin, I would ask you to draw your ideal therapeutic environment. Let your imagination guide you as you consider your ideal office space, walking path, or outdoor meeting space. If you have colored pencils available (or can borrow some crayons from your kids), have fun drawing your ideal therapeutic space. Give yourself 15 or 20 minutes for this part of the exercise. When you are done drawing, look at what nature elements you've included. Imagine what it would be like to actually work in this environment.

The second part of this exercise brings us back to the reality of our current working space. It can be useful to periodically assess your office space or any space you work as a clinician. If you are currently meeting clients outdoors, it is important to look at the affordances of the space and determine what is potentially healing about being in that environment. We'll explore those questions fully in Chapter 6 when we discuss moving therapy outdoors.

For now, take a look at your indoor office space. Walk into your office with *beginner's mind*—as though you are seeing it for the first time. What do you notice first? What draws your attention? What does it feel like to be in the space? What do you find attractive? Off-putting? Inviting? Uncomfortable? Look around for what natural elements are currently included in your office? What is the view from the window(s) in the space? Can windows be open to get fresh air? What kind of natural light is available? What are the sources of artificial lighting in the room? Are there plants in the office and are they healthy looking? Notice the colors and textures of furniture, walls, and flooring. Do they complement one another and create a calm atmosphere? Take note of any nature art or imagery. Can you find any fractal patterns present? What sounds do you hear? What is the noise level in the building or from the outside street? Are there nature sounds present? Which of your senses are stimulated? When your clients are talking with you, what do they see behind you?

These questions are designed to help you look critically and creatively at the space. You may have other questions arise that are unique to your work space. After answering these questions, you might consider revisiting the drawing you created of your ideal healing environment. Are there aspects from the drawing you can incorporate into your current office? Can you think of how you might invite more of the natural world into your therapeutic space?

Most clinicians spend a considerable amount of time in their office. Not only do we need to be concerned with creating a restorative, inviting space for our clients, but we need to be mindful of how the space may contribute to our own sense of well-being and resilience.

RESTORATIVE EFFECTS OF VICARIOUS NATURE

In 2017, my colleagues and I published an article in the journal *Frontiers in Ecology and the Environment* that reported our findings on a yearlong study we had undertaken to understand the impact of vicarious nature experience (e.g., nature videos) on people living in a severely nature-deprived environment (e.g., male inmates in solitary confinement in a state prison). Based on categories outlined by Kellert (2002), we highlighted three ways we might engage with nature:

1. *Direct contact* involves actual physical contact with wilder nature where there is opportunity for multisensorial interactions between humans and other life.
2. *Indirect contact* involves much of the same but occurs in more domestic environments such as our backyards or a city park.
3. *Vicarious nature experience* occurs in the absence of physical contact with natural settings, but includes activities like watching nature videos, reading magazines like *National Geographic*, appreciating nature art or nature photography, and listening to recorded nature sounds such as birdsong or water sounds.

All three types of nature experiences have applicability to ecotherapy and have been shown to have some benefit in reducing stress, anxiety, irritability, and aggression to varying degrees. People experiencing direct and indirect contact reap the greatest benefits, but vicarious experiences with nature have been shown to provide micro-restorative benefits. Recall the previously cited studies by Roger Ulrich (1984) of patients recovering from gall bladder surgery found that increased contact with nature through views of vegetation through their hospital window resulted in faster recovery, a reduction in the use of pain medication, fewer negative notes by nurses, and higher reported patient satisfaction.

Another health care design study by Ulrich is described by Kellert (2012). Ulrich also studied patients and visitors to a hospital emergency room before and after its redesign to include biophilic features. This emergency room was noted for its high levels of stress and aggressive behavior by patients toward hospital staff. The original emergency room was a windowless space with plain white walls, florescent lighting, and spartan, artificial furnishings. The redesigned ER included an aesthetically attractive wall mural of plants and animals in a colorful landscape, natural fiber chairs and carpeting, furnishings that made use of organic shapes, and some vegetation. It is notable that this redesign mainly included symbolic and representational expressions of nature rather than any increase in contact with

natural elements, and the room remained windowless. The researchers reported a significant reduction in stress, hostility, and aggressive behavior among people using the emergency room following
the redesign.

In my study of the effects of nature imagery on inmates in solitary
confinement referenced above, we compared the reported emotions
and behaviors of inmates who had the opportunity to watch nature
videos in the indoor exercise room to those inmates who did not have
that option. Inmates who watched the nature videos reported feeling significantly calmer, less irritable, and better able to regulate their
behavior and had a more positive relationship with staff. Prison staff
corroborated these findings and found the nature imagery to be an
effective intervention to de-escalate behavior and avoid potential violent infractions. Over the 1-year period of the study, inmates who
viewed the nature videos committed 26% fewer violent infractions as
compared to those who did not have access to the videos (Nadkarni
et al., 2017).

Studies are being conducted to investigate whether vicarious nature
experience utilizing Virtual Reality technology can elicit beneficial
effects similar to natural environments for specific populations with
limited access to real nature. This might be of interest to clinicians
who work with special populations.

As we find ourselves increasingly removed from the natural world,
we are looking at ways to include nature—even vicarious nature—
into our daily lives. Vicarious nature experiences are a good supple-
ment to real, direct nature experiences. They provide micro-restorative
benefits in situations where nature contact is not possible. One cau-
tionary note might be that we should be careful that vicarious nature
experiences do not become convenient substitutes for real nature
interactions that engage all our senses, activate our inherent biophilic
tendencies, and offer moments of wonder and awe.

PART II

The Practice of Ecotherapy

5

THE SELF IN AN
ECOLOGICAL CONTEXT

On a bright, clear morning in February 2001, I found myself bobbing in the warm, crystal clear waters of Mexico's Laguna San Ignacio in a six-passenger rubber zodiac (also known as a panga). Gray whales migrate here each winter to calve and raise their young before making the long journey north in the spring. I was on a weeklong whale watching trip with my family, housed in a small fishing boat turned whale watching boat, captained by one of only two American captains allowed in these waters during calving season. A gray whale and her calf approached our small panga. We noticed that the mama whale had maneuvered the calf away from a rowdy group of juvenile male whales that were nearby. She was using our panga as a shield from the group and kept the calf between our rubber boat and herself. There was an instance when the baby whale swam under the panga and we could feel her long body move beneath us. After several minutes of watching the interactions of the whales, we noticed how curious the baby whale seemed to be. It repeatedly swam to the panga and bumped it or bobbed to the surface for a better look. Once the rowdy gang of juveniles swam away, the mama whale seemed to relax. She swam closer to the panga and she seemed to see me sitting in the bow seat. She swam even closer and stared. I extended my hand and sat very still. She moved upward to touch my hand and I felt the cool, rubbery skin and the rough barnacles clustered in places on her enormous head. She had a distinctive orange crescent of whale lice on her forehead. She seemed to seek physical connection between us. I felt compelled to make eye contact with her, so I lifted my prescription sunglasses onto the top of my head. My two eyes met her one large near eye and held its gaze. After what seemed like a long time, she came up out of the water, bumped my head with hers, and knocked my glasses off and into the sea. The moment held a magical quality for me. Losing those glasses was a small price to pay for the deep connection I experienced with that magnificent creature. I was flooded with a deep sense of gratitude for the kinship, the experience of interbeing I felt with the whale. It is an experience that I can vividly recall years later.

My encounter with the gray whale and the resulting feelings surrounding the interconnection I felt with her are an example of Schroeder's (2012) "felt sense" and the ecological Self. These profound interactions with the Other in nature stay with us. They give meaning to life, influence our worldviews, and contribute to how we see ourselves within the context of the bigger world—the more-than-human world. In other words, these interactions contribute to our environmental identity.

This chapter examines how humans develop an environmental identity and why it is important for the individual's well-being, as well as for the health of the planet. A 2009 study reported a correlation between the amount of time spent in nature and people's reported connection to nature (Hinds & Sparks, 2009). Research suggests that a strong sense of nature connectedness is correlated with life satisfaction, psychological well-being, positive and negative emotions (Nisbet et al., 2011), creative and innovative thinking (Leong et al., 2014), and pro-environmental behavior (Hedlund-de Witt, 2013). A 2004 study found that participants who felt the strongest connection to nature were more likely to hold global and environmental concerns (Schultz et al., 2004).

We will begin by exploring the historical roots of humans within the natural world and then discuss how one's environmental identity is influenced by the worldviews and culture of childhood. Several therapeutic tools designed to explore a client's environmental identity will be introduced including the eco-history interview, the eco-genogram, and a place-mapping exercise, and several standardized scales will be considered. The current research on nature connectedness, a component of environmental identity, will be highlighted. In preparation for moving therapy outdoors and for writing nature prescriptions, we will discuss how intentional nature interactions can be facilitated by *active noticing* as a therapeutic activity. The experiences of awe, humility, and a felt sense will be discussed as part of the ecological Self. As clinicians begin to take the ecological context into account, it becomes clear that many of the individual's issues are deeply interconnected with the larger processes occurring on the planet.

THE HISTORICAL ROOTS OF OUR RELATIONSHIP WITH THE NATURAL WORLD

According to the renowned marine scientist and author, Sylvia Earle (1995), life began in the sea 3.5 billion years ago. Life prospered on land half as long and our distant primate ancestors emerged 65 million years ago. Our history as humans began about 5 million years ago. Roots of our modern civilization began about 10 thousand years ago as the last Ice Age gave way to more temperate conditions. During this 10-thousand-year period, the human population increased in number from thousands to millions. It took our species' entire history to produce one billion people by 1800. By 1930 there were two billion, and within 50 years humans numbered four billion. According to the World Population Clock, there are approximately 8.1 billion of us in 2024. Our soaring population may suggest success as a species, but the environmental impact of modern civilization on the planet's ecosystems is profound.

As we reflect on our species' evolution, it becomes clear that we need nature for our physical and psychological well-being. Our bodies and minds came of age embedded in and interacting with the natural world. This evolutionary process shaped the contours of what it means for humans to flourish. Yet we seem to have forgotten that this so. This forgetting and the resulting disconnection from long-standing patterns of interaction with nature have set in motion our widening separation from it. Louv (2008) refers to this widening gap between people and nature as *nature-deficit disorder* and states that a decrease in the time spent outdoors by children and adults is causing detrimental effects to our physical and psychological health.

Paul Shepard, an early influencer on the field of ecopsychology and author of several books including *Coming Home to the Pleistocene* (1998), traced the impact of human activity on their environment. He pointed to the Paleolithic hunter-gatherer as a model for ecologically balanced societies. Shepard saw the development of agriculture and the domestication of animals, about 12,000 years ago, as the time when civilized humanity began to lose the developmental practices that had functioned for thousands of years. He traced this point in time as when human culture achieved a false sense of separation from their natural habitat. Shepard wrote, "Modern life conceals our inherent need for diverse, wild, natural communities, but it does not alter that need" (p. 134).

We cannot go back to the old way of being in nature because as a world culture we are increasingly scientific, and we have always been and continue to be an increasingly technological species. But deep within us we know that nature's patterns and needs are still with us. People travel long distances to vacation in places of natural beauty. We hike in the mountains, walk along the ocean's edge, enjoy a glass of wine at sunset, and celebrate our companion animals as part of the family. We pay high prices for homes located in places of natural beauty, with water views especially valued. Many people spend their leisure time gardening and birding, hunting and fishing, skiing, or basking in the sun.

Even as modern humans seem to forget that we are a species that evolved as part of the natural world, wilderness guides, who take people out into wilder environs for extended periods of time, observe that culture is only about 3 days deep. They report that participants tend to stop looking at their watch, they slow their pace, and they report feeling more present with increased sensory perception. The reader will recall the *three-day effect* that was mentioned in Chapter 3. The three-day effect refers to the science that explains what happens to brain activity that leads to reduced anxiety, enhanced creativity, and increased focus. When we spend time in the natural environment, away from the noise and stress of modern life, stripped of digital technology, and able to slow our pace of life, we begin to remember our place in the order of things. To rejoin the natural community.

Our species has always had a kinship with the more-than-human world. One of the central challenges of our time is to embrace our kinship with the natural world and integrate it into our scientific culture and our technological selves (Kahn & Hasbach, 2012). Ecotherapy expands the context of care to include our kinship with the more-than-human world. My goal here is to offer an ecological view of the human psyche that will deepen the discourse about how clinicians and healers might approach work with clients in a more comprehensive way—one that takes into account our origins and deep rootedness in the natural world.

THE IMPACT OF WORLDVIEWS AND PARADIGM SHIFTS

A worldview is the lens through which our observations of the world are filtered. Worldview is a word often used interchangeably with paradigm. A paradigm is a conceptual model by which our perception of the world is structured. It provides a picture of reality that has been derived from a cosmology—a story of the universe. Hidden within a paradigm or worldview are beliefs and assumptions that are seldom questioned. Our worldview is composed of the stories about the world that are handed down to us through our culture. These worldviews define how an individual will relate to nature. Does one experience the natural world as a community of beings of which we are a part? Does one feel a kinship with the Other? Or does the individual experience nature only as a resource to be used or consumed? Does a person look at a forest and see an intricate ecosystem full of life, or do they see only the board length of timber?

In *The Passion of the Western Mind* (1993), Richard Tarnas explains how our personal world is shaped by our worldview. How we approach reality is defined by the assumptions we have about that reality, and that in turn shapes reality and feeds it back to us. The subject and the object are deeply implicated in each other. In this sense, it is very important to understand the sources of our worldview—the history of our philosophies, sciences, and religions that have led us to this point and shaped the worldview that we hold.

Exploring a client's worldview as it relates to the natural world is unique to the practice of ecotherapy. Most of psychology sees the concept of the self as radically individualistic. Sarah Conn (1998), a clinical psychologist in private practice and early adopter of eco-therapeutic practices, points out that all three major forces in psychology—humanistic, psychoanalytic, and behavioral—see the individual as a bounded, masterful agent, separate from the outside world. This view is reflected in the *Diagnostic and Statistical Manual of Mental Disorders* (*DSM-V-TR*) that practitioners refer to for diagnoses. The *DSM-V-TR* is almost exclusively individualistic in its orientation, contributing to the tendency to pathologize personal pain rather than link it to a larger context. One notable exception is the specifier "with seasonal pattern" that can be applied to the pattern of major depressive episodes in the category of major depressive disorder, recurrent. The essential feature of this diagnosis is the onset and the remission of a major depressive episode at characteristic times of the year, most often beginning in the fall or winter and remitting in the spring.

By contrast, the holistic perspective of ecopsychology involves interdependence and integration of the individual with the more-than-human world. From this perspective, we experience our ecological self when we feel the connection between Self and Other, like the experience I described earlier between myself and the gray whale. This experience can foster a deep sense of belonging, a resonance with other life and sense of place, and a connection to the larger ecological context of planet and cosmos. Thich Nhat Hanh, the Vietnamese Buddhist scholar and teacher, offers a Buddhist view of the relationship between Self and nature in his concept of interbeing. We cannot just *be* by ourselves alone; we exist interconnected with everything else (Nhat Hanh, 1991, p. 95).

Clinicians are seeing more and more clients linking their feelings of anxiety and depression with concerns related to climate change, species loss, and fear about the future of the planet.

ENVIRONMENTAL IDENTITY

Clayton and Opotow (2003) adopted the term *environmental identity* to refer to the inclusion of aspects of nature in a person's self-concept. Environmental identity is defined as a sense of connection to some part of nonhuman nature, based on history, emotional attachment, and/or similarity that affects the ways in which we perceive and act toward the world. One way to think about environmental identity is how we define the natural world including:

- The degree of similarity we perceive between ourselves and other beings in nature.
- Whether we consider nature and the nonhuman world to have intrinsic value. In other words, does nonhuman nature have standing as valued components of our social and moral community?

Our environmental identity affects our worldview and vice versa. Do we see nature only as a resource for our use—holding a mechanistic view? Or do we see nature as family, where humans are part of the larger family of the natural world—holding a kinship view?

A pioneer in psychoanalytic treatment, psychiatrist Harold Searles (1960) argued that the human relationship with the natural world is transcendentally important and a part of our psychological well-being. This broadened conception of identity would include how individuals see themselves in the ecological context, how they view animate and inanimate nature, how people relate to the natural world, and how they relate to each other in the context of larger environmental issues (Clayton & Opotow, 2003).

As an ecotherapist, it is important to understand clients' worldview on these topics and understand how they experience their environmental identity. Like other forms of social identity, environmental identity tends to be implicit unless one is asked about it. Here we look at several methods of inquiry.

The Eco-History Interview

One method to investigate a client's environmental identity is through a short series of questions about their eco-history. Consider the following questions to get the discussion started:

1. Where were you raised? (farm, small town, suburbs, city)
2. What were your most memorable childhood experiences with nature?
3. Did you tend a garden or care for animals that were raised for food?
4. Did you have pets?
5. Did you learn to enjoy being outdoors or did you fear or avoid the outdoors?
6. How did these experiences influence your present feelings and relationship to nature?
7. What do you recall about your parents', grandparents', siblings', or other important adults' attitudes about relating to the natural world?

I will sometimes ask clients to reflect on the discussion and consider:

1. How has my eco-history and my worldview influenced my relationship with the natural world?
2. What is my vision or hope for paradigm change at the personal and collective level?

The Eco-Genogram

Another method practitioners can use to include the client's relationship history with the natural world is to expand the traditional genogram. The traditional genogram is a drawing of the client's family tree that explores the significant family relationships. This drawing is a useful method to better understand the client's family of origin and the dynamics among the family members. A genogram usually includes several generations. In contrast to the human-centric focus of the geno-gram, the eco-genogram also includes the place(s) the person grew up that was meaningful to them; animals that were a part of their life; and land features such a river, mountain, lake, or forest that were integral to their childhood. The eco-genogram can be completed by the client during a session or assigned as homework, then discussed in the subse-quent session. Including the animals, land features, and special places in a client's early life gives a fuller, richer understand of their life story. The illustration that follows includes the elements of a traditional geno-gram and adds other important influences in the client's life. In this illustration, the client (labeled "Me") identified the major influences in her life that contributed to her relationship with the natural world. She explained that her grandmother, her mother, her uncle, and a neighbor

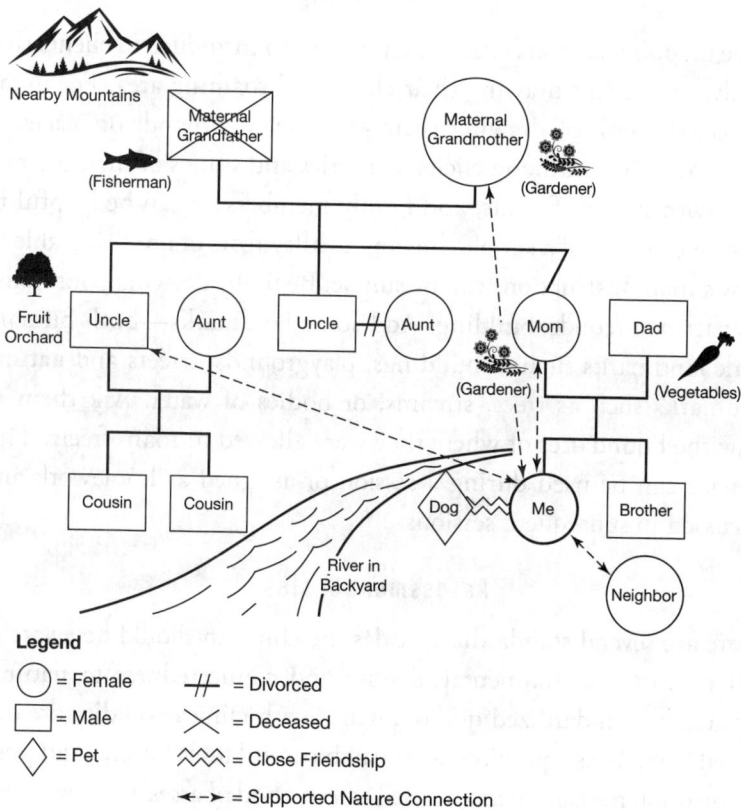

Figure 5.1 An Eco-Genogram

supported her connection to nature. She noted that they were all gardeners of various types and she identified herself as a gardener now. She shared that her dog, that she had from age 10 to age 21, was her "best friend." The family often went camping in the mountains and these trips often included her cousins, with whom she is still close. She also spent time at the river that ran behind her home. She said she went there often as a teen "to just think and be alone." She noted that her dad had a vegetable garden and she attributed "growing up eating well" and learning to enjoy a variety of foods at an early age to his garden. It was curious to me that she did not include her dad as supporting a nature connection, and I inquired about that. She said she didn't have a particularly close relationship with him growing up, and that led to additional discussion in the therapeutic process.

Place Mapping

Place mapping is an exercise the clinician can introduce to clients that involves the client drawing their childhood roaming area. For many people, the task of drawing their yard, neighborhood, or places of importance in childhood elicits memories and stories of their interactions with nature, friends, and family members. It can be helpful to have an example of a simple drawing to allay fears of not being able to draw a map. Instructions can be simple: Begin by drawing your house or apartment/condo building. Add some landmarks—both human-made landmarks such as buildings, playgrounds, streets and natural landmarks such as trees, streams, or bodies of water. Ask them to draw the boundaries of where they were allowed to roam freely. This exercise can be used during a session or assigned as homework and discussed in subsequent sessions.

Assessment Scales

There are several standardized scales the clinician should be aware of that measure environmental identity and connectedness to natural. Two of the standardized questionnaires with clinical validity are discussed here. These questionnaires can be useful tools for pre- and post-intervention measurements, as well as a method of assessing how much the client identifies with the natural world. As we consider moving therapy outdoors, it is important to understand the client's previous experience in nature, their expressed preferences of natural landscapes, and their motivation to include nature in the therapeutic process.

The Environmental Identity Scale (EID) was developed by Clayton and Opotow (2003) to assess the extent to which the natural environment plays an important role in a person's self-definition. The original scale includes 24 items with a seven-point Likert scale as an answer format. It measures five aspects of EID:

1. The salience of identity—indicating the extent and significance of an individual's interactions with nature
2. Self-identification is assessed through the way in which nature contributes to the collective to which the individual belongs
3. Ideology is measured by support for environmental education and sustainable lifestyle choices
4. The positive emotions are measured by asking about the enjoyment one derives in nature
5. An autobiographical component comprising of memories of interactions with nature is included

The EID Scale measures and provides evidence for individual differences in the strength with which a person perceives this identity as part of their self-concept. Evidence suggests that early experiences in nature, particularly with significant others, can have a powerful impact on the formation of an environmental identity in children. In 2021, Clayton proposed the Revised EID Scale, which aimed to have items more inclusive of broader populations and nature experiences. The revised scale is designed to be more applicable to urban and cross-cultural populations (Clayton, Czellar et al., 2021).

The Connectedness to Nature Scale (CNS) was designed by Mayer and Franz (2004) to measure an individual's trait levels of feeling emotionally connected to the natural world. It is designed to tap an individual's affective, experiential connection to nature. This scale is comprised of 14 items with a five-point Likert scale as an answer format. The scale may be useful to practitioners to evaluate whether interventions aimed at increasing nature contact actually elevate the client's sense of feeling connected to nature.

As a clinician, think about how you might assess your clients' environmental identity and their connectedness to nature. Which of the activities or assessment scales mentioned above seem to fit with the population with which you work? Consider your own reactions to broadening the lens with which you view your clients to include the ecological context of their lives.

ACTIVE NOTICING AS A THERAPEUTIC TOOL

The psychological construct of nature connectedness provides a focal point for understanding the human–nature relationship. Recent research has shown that a high level of nature connectedness helps to explain pro-nature conservation efforts, as well as pro-environmental behaviors associated with addressing issues related to climate change. The benefits of higher levels of nature connectedness extend to human well-being; systematic reviews and meta-analyses show a clear link between nature connection and mental well-being, and interventions suggest a causal link between nature connectedness and improved mental health. Reflecting this growing evidence, nature connectedness has been proposed as a basic psychological need and a key metric within well-being assessments (Richardson et al., 2022).

Given the importance of nature connectedness for humans' and nature's well-being, clinicians need to understand more about specific forms of engagement with nature that promote nature connectedness. Here it is important to make the distinction between nature exposure and nature experience. As discussed in earlier chapters, there is a large body of research that demonstrates a relationship between nature exposure and human well-being. Researchers continue to learn more about how soft fascination contributes to restoring directed attention fatigue. This research has provided evidence to support policies and recommendations leading to more equitable access to green space and lends support for spending time in the outdoors.

Empirical research has shown that nature connectedness and

mental well-being can be improved through interventions that prompt people to actively notice and appreciate nature. The evidence suggests that although just spending time in nature is beneficial for a sense of well-being, what matters more is what people do with that time and how those activities strengthen their relationship with the natural world (Richardson et al., 2022).

As an ecotherapist, it is important to promote *intentional* interactions between the client and nature. Activities that stimulate the senses can encourage the client to be fully present and mindfully engaged. We might actively notice nature by observing the beauty of a sunset, listening to the patterns of birdsong, feeling the sand under our feet at the beach or feeling the soil in our hands in the garden, tasting the salty air by the ocean, or smelling the fragrance of the forest after a rainfall. These are examples of highly sensual experiences in nature that promote profound emotions such as compassion, a sense of belonging, gratitude, and wonder. These intentional interactions engage a person on a physical, emotional, spiritual, or intellectual level. These are experiences that help one to feel fully alive and connected with one's ecological Self.

For well-being, pro-environmental behaviors, and nature connectedness, there is clearly a need for active sensory engagement with nature while outdoors rather than simply being passively exposed to it (Richardson et al., 2022). This perspective becomes central to the work of the ecotherapist as they formulate treatment plans that involve moving sessions outdoors and write nature prescriptions for clients. Active noticing and intentional engagement with nature will be elaborated on in the upcoming chapters. Specifically, the next chapter discusses being intentional about the kind of nature engagement the clinician considers when the therapy session moves outdoors, and Chapter 7 looks at the importance of specificity in writing nature prescriptions.

THE ECOLOGICAL SELF IN PRACTICE

The field of positive psychology focuses on the character strengths and behaviors that allow individuals to build a life of meaning and purpose—to move beyond surviving to flourishing. Theorists and researchers in the field have sought to identify the elements of a good life, examining what improves life satisfaction, supports resilience, and fosters a sense of well-being. One of those elements of a good life is a sense of belonging—of being a part of something bigger than ourself. From a societal point of view, this is often experienced by identifying with a group such as a faith community, a particular neighborhood, a favorite sports team, or our extended family or clan.

But in recent decades, a growing number of people report feeling lonely and isolated. According to a 2023 report titled, "Our Epidemic of Loneliness and Isolation: The U.S. Surgeon General's Advisory on the Healing Effects of Social Contact and Community" about 50% of adults in America reported experiencing loneliness, with some of the highest rates among young adults. Studies indicate that loneliness and isolation are more widespread than many of the other major health concerns we face such as smoking, diabetes, and obesity and present comparable levels of risk to health and premature death. Further, social isolation is associated with increased risk for anxiety, depression, and dementia (Office of the U. S. Surgeon General, 2023).

Social connection is a fundamental human need, as essential to survival as food, water, and shelter. Our brains are wired to live in proximity to others. Our ancestors relied on each other to help them meet their basic needs. Despite the technological advances that now allow us to live without engaging with others (e.g., food delivery, online banking, remote work, and remote entertainment), our biological need to connect remains.

Author Richard Louv (2019) points to another possible source of our sense of loneliness and isolation—species loneliness—a term he describes as "the gnawing fear that we are alone in the universe with a desperate hunger for connection with other life" (p. 16). Louv uses the analogy of what happens when an individual is cut off from social contact with other people—they are left more vulnerable, are susceptible to depression, and are more easily controlled. Similarly, as we lose our kinship with the more-than-human world, we lose our sense of comfort, belonging, and compassion and that sense of being a part of something much bigger than ourselves.

Depending on the individual, the transcendent Other may exist objectively "out there"—grounded in a deep sense of place, experienced in a memorable interaction with another being, viewed in the extraordinary beauty of a mountain landscape or the intricacy of a rose, or moved by the vastness of the seas. For others, the transcendent Other may be experienced as part of human culture such as feeling a deep sense of community or conceptualized in traditional religious terms. Regardless of how it is imagined, the experience of the Other gives meaning to one's life and helps define who one is in relation to the world. The experience of the Other is felt at a level deeper than the intellectual level, and it is more than an abstract thought or concept. It may be difficult to express in words, but it is felt in the heart and may stir powerful emotions (Schroeder, 1992). Experiences of this kind can occur in a variety of contexts. For many people, the natural world seems to be a primary setting for spiritual experiences, peak experiences, and moments of awe and wonder. The ecological Self is touched in these experiences. The embodied cognition and felt sense of deep connection to all life that I experienced with the gray whale encounter is but one example.

As clinicians it is important to understand the deeper aspects of our clients' being: what gives their life meaning and groundedness, especially in our rapidly changing world. Ecotherapy expands the lens of inquiry to include exploration about and validation for the ecological Self.

6

INCORPORATING NATURE-
BASED METHODS INTO
YOUR PRACTICE

Practicing clinicians who attend my workshops on incorporating eco-therapy methods into their work are often surprised to realize that they are already using some nature-based techniques in their office setting. Intuitively we know that nature is good for us and it is often reflected in how we create healing spaces. In this chapter, we will explore how to be intentional about it. Research into the therapeutic and restorative benefits of contact with nature has looked at three main contact points: viewing nature, being in the presence of nearby nature, and active participation and involvement in nature. We will explore how to incorporate ecotherapeutic methods into a broad spectrum of settings including the traditional therapy office, outdoors in local nearby nature, and moving into wilder environs.

I'll begin by introducing the therapeutic triadic relationship of therapist, client, and nature. The expansion of the intake session to include questions that broaden the scope of treatment to include the ecological aspect of the client's life will be discussed. We will also discuss various ways to invite nature into the office—through biophilic design, by utilizing the nature basket in therapy, and by making use of nature imagery. The chapter concludes with a discussion about moving therapy sessions outdoors. We will highlight the importance of identifying the therapeutic purpose, discuss some of the unique features of outdoor therapy, discuss how to prepare the client for moving sessions outdoors, and look at incorporating nature-based methods into treatment planning.

ECOTHERAPY FOR A VARIETY OF THERAPEUTIC SETTINGS

Despite the compelling body of evidence about the positive benefits of interactions with nature, some clinicians and clients can be overwhelmed by the idea of incorporating nature into therapy. Some fear that they must pack up and move out into wilderness settings to practice ecotherapy. Others may experience fears about being outdoors at all—concerns about bug bites, injury, and encounters with wild animals—are all reasons that may keep people indoors. But hopefully the reader has a better understanding of ecotherapy as they have navigated to this point in the book. Remember that ecotherapy is about expanding the lens with which we see the client to include their relationship with the natural world. Accurately assessing the client's relationship with nature, understanding the history of that relationship, and gauging the client's openness to engaging with nature is key to successfully including the natural world as a therapeutic partner.

As discussed earlier in this book, more and more clients are coming to the therapy office with anxiety and depression related to climate change and the environmental situation. When the therapist asks about their relationship and engagement with nature, it opens the door to exploring these topics that the client may have assumed were beyond the scope of therapy. Similarly, ecotherapy challenges the clinician to recognize and address the chronic stressors and emotions that are in response to the gradual effects of our changing environment that may not be articulated by clients.

Nature-based methods are at home in the office setting. Since many clinical offices are situated in urban centers, clinicians can explore how to invite nature indoors and they can offer nature prescriptions—homework assignments—to get clients connected with their local green or blue space. Ecotherapy can also be offered in local, nearby settings. Moving outdoors in an urban setting usually involves *walk and talk* sessions in a park or green space, or sitting by a river, body of water, or in a garden. Ecotherapy sessions can also be offered in wilder environments that might involve hiking on trails, walking or sitting together in a forest setting, or even overnight group work that moves into the special fields of adventure therapy or wilderness therapy. We'll explore how to incorporate nature-based methods in the office and nearby nature settings in this chapter, and discuss the various forms ecotherapy can take when moving outdoors further afield in Chapter 9.

THE TRIADIC RELATIONSHIP

The triadic relationship in ecotherapy refers to the therapeutic relationship between the therapist, the client, and nature. Let's begin by highlighting what are the specific components of a traditional therapeutic relationship between the therapist and the client. What is unique about the therapeutic relationship?

- A therapeutic relationship involves *active listening* by the therapist.
- The therapist stays aware of the *nonverbal communication* by the client.
- The relationship offers *unconditional positive regard* to the client.
- The therapist is *skilled in listening deeply* to what is being said and not said.
- The therapist makes *observations at critical junctions* and asks questions accordingly.
- Both the therapist and the client are *fully present* to the process.
- There is *a therapeutic intimacy* that can form as thoughts and feelings are shared by the client.
- The relationship is *unidirectional*—the therapist is there for the client, not the other way around.
- The relationship is governed by a *code of ethics*.

As a practitioner, you can add to this list of components of a therapeutic relationship. Ecotherapy includes all these aspects of traditional therapy and incorporates nature into the process to deepen the work by:

- Engaging in direct interactions with the natural environment by moving sessions outdoors or through nature prescriptions—assignments between therapy sessions. More on nature prescriptions in Chapter 7.
- Including natural objects as prompts in the office setting. (The nature basket will be discussed later in this chapter.)
- Incorporating nature metaphors in the therapeutic dialogue.
- Making use of nature imagery in the office and in guided meditations.
- Including the concept of a sense of place that fosters a sense of belonging.
- Expanding the client's perspective on the presenting issues when therapy moves outdoors.
- Focusing on sensorial awareness and embodied cognition.
- Including biophilic design in the office setting.
- Attuning to the potential social and emotional impacts of climate change and environmental concerns that might be an underlying factor for the client.

THE INTAKE SESSION

During the initial session, the therapist learns about the issues or concerns that brought the client into therapy. We gather information about the client's physical and mental health, their education and work history, their current living situation, and their family of origin. To better understand the broader context of nature in a client's life, ecotherapists weave in several nature-oriented questions into the intake interview. In my practice, I generally ask:

1. Can you tell me about a memory you have of being in nature as a child?

2. How did your family of origin view the natural world?

3. What do you like to do outdoors at this point in your life, and how often do you get to do it?

4. How much time have you spent in nature during the past week?

Answers to these questions provide initial information about the clients' historical and current relationship with nature and the ways that they orient to it, value it, and engage with it (Hasbach, 2012). Clients will often share stories about a favorite pet, a special memory of working in the garden with a grandparent, a painful recollection of hiding in the woods outside their childhood home to avoid family strife or violence, grief over the loss of a beloved place to development or wildfire, and stories of awe, fear, compassion, and love for the non-human Other.

As important, these discussions make the clients' experiences of the natural world and their concerns related to climate change (e.g., stories in the news, weather events, species extinction) relevant to therapy and lay the foundation for future discussions and nature prescriptions (Hasbach, 2015).

ECOTHERAPY IN THE CLINICAL OFFICE

When we discussed restorative environments in Chapter 4, you had the opportunity to assess your office space for its restorative effect, using a series of questions. Clinicians can be very creative in finding ways to enrich their office space with nature: positioning furniture so that the client has a view of the outdoors; hanging artwork with nature images, utilizing natural materials, colors and textures; including healthy plants and natural light in the space; and adding water sounds from a small table fountain. Even shared office space can be enhanced by a vase of cut flowers or having a few natural objects strategically placed within reach or view of where the client is seated.

The Nature Basket

One nature-based technique I have found impactful is the nature basket. I keep a small basket of found nature objects in my office containing shells, small rocks, seed pods, sticks, mosses, leaves, and feathers. Items are intentionally selected that could provide metaphors or clear representations of feelings. Examples include a rock that is dark on one side and almost white on the other; a shell in the shape of a spiral, a seed pod with jagged edges, and a well-worn feather. If a client seems stuck or at a loss for words, I'll invite them to look at the objects in the basket to see if there is an item to which they are drawn. Often, they will select an object that provides the visual prompt they need to share their thoughts or feelings.

Elsewhere I have written about a particularly powerful example of how this technique was utilized with a client who came to see me for depression and other issues related to the breakup of an important relationship. She was having difficulty finding her words to express what she was feeling. When given the opportunity to select an item from the nature basket, she chose a vine that had formed a hollow ball. She said that it represented the emptiness she felt inside and the "tangled mess" of her life. The vine ball provided a useful prop for her to articulate her feelings (Hasbach, 2012, 2015, 2016).

Another client who was expressing a great deal of frustration over an encounter with a coworker was asked to look in the nature basket to see if there was an item he was drawn to that represented his part in the situation. He selected the two-tone stone and said it reminded him of his tendency to have black-and-white thinking. The self-awareness of his own tendency was brought forward without judgment and allowed him to reexamine his behavior and its impact on the situation.

A client who came to see me after the loss of her husband was processing her grief. In one of our early sessions, she sat for a long time without saying anything. I asked her to look in the basket to see if anything there represented what she was feeling. She chose a weather-worn stick, and said it "appeared to be old and it had been through a lot." This opened discussion about aging and loss and her feelings of moving forward in life without her spouse.

MAKING USE OF NATURE METAPHORS

These examples of how natural objects from the nature basket were effective as props for the client also represent good examples of nature metaphors. Clinicians have long recognized the importance of metaphor as a tool for deeper understanding and growth. Metaphors frame our understanding of one thing that is known or easily recognized to another thing that is new or perhaps challenging to articulate. In *Metaphors We Live By,* Lakeoff and Johnson (1981) offer many examples of how everyday language is filled with metaphors that we may not always notice.

Clinicians who practice ecotherapy listen for metaphors that clients use that come from nature and sometimes include nature metaphors to deepen the therapeutic discussion. A few years ago, I was working with a successful middle-aged man in a stable marriage who was experiencing mild depression and feelings of "being bored with life." He talked about his tendency to always make the safe decision, always taking the middle of the road, in his personal and professional life. Knowing he was an avid hiker from previous discussions, I asked him about trails he hiked and about his experiences of walking mountain trails that are sometimes narrow. We talked about what it meant to him to get to edges when hiking. He shared how he felt more alive and aware and present when he was walking an edge or ridgeline versus walking the middle of a wider path or logging road. We came back to that discussion of edges and centers many times as he explored the safe decisions he was prone to make and what it meant to him to take calculated risks.

The natural world that surrounds us offers many metaphors that help us to see our connection to patterns of growth, healing, and the cycle of life. Many practitioners of horticulture therapy find the cycle of the garden offers powerful metaphors for life. In addition to the ones shared from my practice above, other metaphors I've heard from clients or used in therapy include: sinking in quicksand, swimming upstream, feeling bright and sunny, feeling dark, standing on shaky ground, being left high and dry, and so on. These outer mappings of inner landscapes provide rich descriptors and powerful conduits to meaningful discussion and insight.

Making Use of Nature Imagery

Just as powerful as nature-based metaphor, nature imagery in the therapeutic space can have powerful impact on clients' experience. A study conducted in an in-patient psychiatric hospital revealed that the subject of art used on the walls influenced patient behavior. Abstract artwork was often defaced or destroyed by these patients, while nature art was not.

Nature images allow us to remain connected to the natural world while we are indoors. A large body of research shows that the presence of nature art or nature videos in health care settings can have a positive effect on patients. In Chapter 2 we discussed how one study highlighted the impact of a nature mural in the waiting room of a dental office. On the days the mural was present, dental patients reported less anxiety and had lower blood pressure than the patients with appointments on the days the mural was not present. Another study looked at the effects of displaying different ceiling-mounted pictures to presurgical patients who were lying on gurneys in the holding area of a hospital surgical suite. One picture depicted a quiet, natural scene that included water; another showed a sailboarder leaning into the wind; and another had no picture at all. Findings showed that after a brief exposure of 3 to 6 minutes, patients who viewed the serene nature picture had systolic blood pressure levels that were 10–15 points lower than those who viewed the other two pictures.

In reviewing many studies on the effects of health care environmental design, Ulrich (2001) concluded that as a general guideline clinicians should choose representational pictures showing serene, spatially open nature and settings with water or parklike areas. He suggested avoiding chaotic abstract art, surreal art, and works containing incongruous elements and scenes containing little depth or openness.

Following research-based guidelines can help the practitioner choose the best nature images for their office or clinic. A 2003 study by Ulrich and Gilpin identified the five best types of art for healing environments:

1. *Calm, slow-moving water.* Water is necessary for life. Studies found that calm, slow-moving water can make patients feel at ease and can lower heart rate.
2. *Lush green vegetation and flowers.* Lush vegetation is symbolic of life, health, and growth. Flowers have long been prized for their beauty and evoke feelings of hope, joy, and gratitude.
3. *Open landscapes.* Sweeping landscape images have outranked urban images in numerous studies that looked at which photographs lower stress in study participants. Openness in the foreground of an image invites the viewer into the image, which has been shown to increase the person's engagement with the image.
4. *Park-like or savannah-like images.* As we discussed in Chapter 2, humans are drawn to savannah views due to our evolutionary history. Those images that include trees and open space answer our deep need for refuge and security. Such images offer a sense of calm and protection and have been shown to lower stress and instill positive feeling.
5. *Nonthreatening wildlife.* Images of birds and nonthreatening wildlife connect us with our deep kinship with other members of the natural world.

In Chapter 4, I mentioned Nooshin Razini, a pediatrician at UCSF Benioff Children's Hospital in Oakland, California, who prescribes nature to the families she works with and offers trainings on nature-based medicine to other pediatricians. She has transformed her clinical office so that nature is everywhere. There are maps and pictures of local wilderness spots on the walls of the clinic so that she can easily talk with families about local parks and outdoor resources. Similarly, many hospitals and physician offices have incorporated the latest research findings on the impact of nature art by including photos of local nature in the hallways, waiting rooms, and patient rooms.

Mental health practitioners are doing the same. Displaying beautiful nature art or playing recurrent nature videos in the waiting room of your office can allow the client to reset their thoughts and prepare for their session. Nature art in the treatment room can add beauty and calm not only to the clients, but also can benefit the practitioner as well. As you consider what art for healing looks like, you'll want to consider where the art will be hung, the population you work with that will be viewing the images, and what feelings the images evoke.

Nature imagery can also be incorporated into guided meditations. Here is it important to understand the client's experience of nature so that you can tailor the nature imagery to what is most appropriate for the particular client. If there is a cultural bias or a personal experience that would lead to stress at the mention of a forest setting, obviously that should be avoided. Understanding what kind of natural environment the client is drawn to or finds restorative can inform the clinician about what to include or avoid in a guided meditation.

We have looked at various ways to bring nature-based methods into the clinical office setting. By asking about the client's relationship with nature during the intake session we make that relationship relevant for therapy. By expanding the scope of treatment to include the human–nature relationship, we invite clients to acknowledge their relationship with the natural world or their feelings of disconnection from it. Expanding our own lens with which we view the client allows the clinician to recognize the etiology of some of the emotions experienced by the client about climate change and the environmental situation. We looked at various ways to invite nature into the office through biophilic design, thoughtful nature imagery and art, and being mindful of what the client looks at when in a session. We discussed making use of nature metaphor in therapeutic dialogue and by creating a nature basket of natural objects.

We introduced the triadic relationship of therapist, client, and nature. The next section addresses nature as a partner in the therapeutic process as we move sessions outdoors.

Moving Therapy Outdoors

Many of the nature-based methods and practices of ecotherapy invite a reconnection with real nature and the wilder Self. A part of our inner wisdom or deep knowing can be accessed if we are willing to move out into the natural world and experience it fully and mindfully. Ecotherapists invite clients to take the therapeutic work outdoors through nature prescriptions to do between sessions and/ or by accompanying clients outdoors during the therapy session. Like all decisions clinicians make regarding client care, it is important to identify the therapeutic purpose of going outdoors. As we do so, it is important to keep in mind some of the unique features of outdoor therapy:

- Direct experience in nature affords heightened sensorial experiences and perceptions that connect the inner world with the outer landscape.
- The pace or rhythm of life may be slowed for a while, allowing for deeper reflection and a felt sense of connection with the natural world.
- The opportunity to be fully present is heightened.
- Through an increased consciousness in their ecological community, clients can widen their circle of identification and become more aware of their sense of place and feelings of belonging to something bigger than themselves.
- There is an opportunity to frame the client's issues within a wider and deeper context. Being outdoors around others can change a client's experience of their emotional struggles by bringing them into immediate awareness of a bigger world.
- Walking side-by-side with their therapist outdoors can lead some clients to feel more empowered than when they are seated across from the therapist in the office.
- Spontaneous interactions with nature often emerge that can influence the client's perspective.
- The place becomes a witness to the client's story and nature becomes a partner in the therapeutic process.
- Outdoor therapy often involves physical movement that can lessen anxiety and depression and contribute to physical wellness. The mind–body connection becomes tangible. Several studies have demonstrated a reduction in tension and stress and an increase in relaxation and sense of calm as study participants moved from urban walking areas into natural areas.

- There is an opportunity for a cocreated therapeutic experience between the therapist and the client.
- New challenges emerge regarding boundary setting, maintaining the asymmetry of the therapeutic relationship, and other ethical concerns that will be addressed in Chapter 9.

Preparing to Move Outdoors

Some ecotherapists meet their clients outdoors after the initial introductory phone conversation. But most ecotherapists meet the client at their office for at least one-to-two sessions before moving sessions outdoors. It is important to understand the client's situation, conduct a thorough intake session, assess the client's appropriateness for outdoor therapy, and discuss issues related to confidentiality, comfort level, physical abilities, and safety issues.

The clinician needs to accept that a client may not want to move outdoors for therapy and would prefer to stay in the office for their session. We discussed earlier how easily nature can be brought into the office setting with a little creativity and thoughtful design. Most ecotherapists have a hybrid practice: many sessions are conducted indoors (at least for part of the year) and clients are given nature prescriptions for activities to do outdoors between sessions. Even clients who are being seen online can be assigned nature prescriptions that enrich the therapeutic experience and add to the therapeutic dialogue. More about nature prescriptions in the next chapter.

If you are taking a client outdoors, there are a few things to keep in mind as you prepare to do so. First, identify and document your purpose for moving therapy outdoors. This helps the clinician focus on the goals for therapy and identify specific features of the outdoor experience that will be therapeutic. For example, walk and talk therapy may be much easier for someone with anxiety, who may find movement more comfortable than sitting in one place for an extended period of time; or for a teen or adolescent who may be uncomfortable sitting in a room across from the clinician, whom they may perceive as an authority figure. The clinician can think about what kinds of human–nature interactions would be most potent to address the client's presenting issues.

It is important to discuss the risks and benefits of moving sessions outdoors with the client. This instills confidence in the client and raises awareness of what is involved. It is the clinician's responsibility to raise concerns that the client may not have thought about. For example, it is important to discuss how the client would like to handle the situation if while you are outdoors you encounter someone you or the client knows. This is obviously a confidentiality concern that needs to be addressed. You might also ask about health concerns such as whether the client is allergic to bees, has any respiratory issues such as asthma or other conditions that may be affected by weather or pollen levels, has any muscular–skeletal limitations, or has other health-related issues that may have come up during the intake session. I have found it is helpful to ask open-ended questions about whether the client has any concerns that I haven't asked about. One client shared with me that she had a fear of dogs and asked if we might encounter dogs on the trail we were planning to walk. Another client asked if she could bring a mat to sit on rather than sit directly on the ground because of her cultural norms.

Information gathered during the preparation phase helps the clinician assess the comfort level and physical abilities of the client. Moving therapy sessions outdoors is not meant to be a physical strain or challenge. It is important to remember that the purpose is to engage with the natural world in an intentional way to deepen and enrich the therapeutic process.

At the end of the preparation discussion, it is a good practice to review your understanding of the client's responses and document the discussion in the chart. Documentation requirements are often determined by the agency or organization where the clinician practices. Private practitioners must decide how best to document the preparation discussion. Some ecotherapists have a checklist of items to go over with the client and ask the client to sign the document acknowledging that the items have been discussed. Others simply document the discussion in the clinical chart. Either way, it is important to document that a safety and concerns discussion occurred, and there is a clear understanding and agreement between the therapist and the client.

If you are moving therapy out to a fairly domestic setting such as a bike path or city park or backyard garden, there is generally little risk involved. But if you are moving the sessions to wilder environments such as a mountain trail, close to moving water, or to environments where there is more unpredictability involved, a thorough discussion of the risks involved needs to take place, and the agreement and understanding documentation is an important consideration.

The clinician should go prepared when meeting with a client outdoors. Even if I am holding a walk and talk session on the nearby bike and walking path at my office, I take a small safety bag with me. I carry my phone, a bottle of water, tissues, and a small first-aid kit. Think about what you would take in a small bag to be prepared for the unexpected. This will be influenced by the environment you are moving into and by the population with which you are working.

Barriers to Moving Therapy Outdoors

For all the benefits of outdoor therapy, there are several logical challenges to consider as the clinician plans to move therapy sessions outdoors. Scheduling concerns, the location of the office and its proximity to green or blue natural space that works for therapy, and unpredictable weather conditions all offer challenges for the practitioner. In my own practice, my office is in a building that is situated in a quiet, wooded area along a walking and biking path that runs adjacent to a river and passes through a local community park. This location offers the opportunity to meet the client in the office and walk right out onto a safe, pleasant walking path to the river or park where we can sit on a bench or walk and talk for a part of our session. But there are few office settings that are so amenable to this practice. Most ecotherapists schedule part of their day in a local park or at a specific outdoor meeting place each week and meet their clients at that designated spot. Others see clients at their home office and have a garden area or outdoor seating area in which to hold sessions (Buzzell, 2009). Other practitioners have a deck or porch at their office to which they can easily move that overlooks green space or water.

Organization policies and agency rules can also influence whether you can meet clients in an outdoor setting. This is especially relevant for schools and agencies that work with children, adolescents, and teens—where there are strict policies of where a child can engage with a counselor or health care provider.

Other barriers to consider include patient physical limitations, the availability of transportation to desirable green or blue space and the time it takes to get there, and the physical safety of the surroundings. The clinician should be mindful of any socioeconomic issues or racial barriers the client may face in accessing natural areas.

INCORPORATING ECOTHERAPY METHODS INTO TREATMENT PLANNING

Research has provided ample evidence that various types of nature experiences result in mental health benefits. Studies have demonstrated beneficial psychological impacts of nature images and sounds. In this chapter, we discussed how clinicians might incorporate both in the office setting.

Experimental fieldwork has shown the benefits of nature experience by contrasting within-group change across affective, cognitive, and physiological dimensions in study participants who walked in natural environments versus urban ones. Clinicians can make use of this evidence as they consider outdoor areas where they might conduct walk and talk sessions with their clients.

Studies demonstrate affective benefits of exposure to nature, particularly on mood regulation. This includes stress reduction and lessening depression symptoms, as well as contributing to positive psychological functioning and resilience. The benefits of nature interaction have been assessed through self-report, psychological measures, biomarkers of stress, and brain responses. These benefits vary in terms of their magnitude and duration—from changes in short-term emotional states to longer term shifts in patterns of mood and thought, to changes in mental health disorders (Bratman et al., 2019). Evidence also suggests that the affective impacts vary by the duration and frequency of the nature exposure, the patterns of human–nature interactions employed, and the characteristics of the environment including the landscape type and the biodiversity available to interact with (Bratman et al., 2021). In this chapter, we discussed the importance of the intake session to initially understand the client's experience of interacting with nature. Gaining a thorough understanding of the client's landscape preferences, comfort level, physical capabilities, cultural-related concerns, and any fears they hold, is vital for planning a successful outdoor session.

Research evidence supports the stress reduction theory that was introduced in Chapter 2. That theory posits that humans have an innate affinity to connect with nature (biophilia) due to our psycho-evolutionary history. Other studies have found correlations between preferred natural environments and positive affect. Over time, pleasant memories and experiences with a specific place can lead to a bond or an emotional attachment to that place that ecotherapists call a sense of place. For some people, this leads to feelings of groundedness and a deep sense of belonging. Clinicians can help clients explore their sense of place—a potential resource available to clients that can be incorporated into nature prescriptions during the course of therapy.

Although many of these findings are correlational, taken together the results are encouraging and point to the powerful impact reconnection with nature can have on our psychological, physiological, and emotional states and sense of well-being. The clinician knowledgeable in the literature and skilled in nature-based methods can add a powerful dimension to the services they offer their clients.

By combining ecotherapy methods with cognitive behavior therapy, person-centered therapy, relational therapy, and other therapeutic modalities, we can deepen the impact of the work, acknowledge the human–nature relationship, and capture the healing qualities of interactions with the natural world. Given the robust body of evidence available today, incorporating nature into therapeutic work can now be considered a component of best practice for patient care.

7

THE NATURE PRESCRIPTION

Imagine a visit with your doctor that concludes with a prescription—not for a medication, but for a 30-minute walk outdoors in nature. Like a drug prescription, the nature prescription is tailored specifically to you based on your physical and psychological history, your presenting concern, and your access to nature that you were asked about earlier at intake. This practice is happening globally and it is becoming more prevalent. Because of the robust body of evidence that supports having contact with nature is good for us physically and psychologically, an increasing number of physicians and mental health professionals are prescribing nature to their patients or clients. Occupational therapists may prescribe horticulture therapy or gardening, pet therapy, and participation at care farms to their patients. Physicians in emergency medicine often lead wilderness therapy groups and adventure therapy groups, and pediatricians are prescribing time in parks and local nature spots to the families with which they work.

It is a common practice among mental health clinicians to assign homework to clients between sessions in order to extend the therapeutic process beyond the session time. This chapter introduces the practice of writing nature-based homework assignments—nature prescriptions—that involve engagement with nature in ways that would be most potent to address the client's specific concerns, issues, and therapeutic process. For clients who prefer to have their therapy sessions in the office and for those clinical practices where it is not practical or possible to move sessions outdoors, nature prescriptions can be a way to invite nature into therapy. Nature prescriptions provide the opportunity for the client to engage with the natural world and bring their experience, insights, and thoughts back to the sessions in the office.

In this chapter, we will look at who is currently writing nature prescriptions and review various programs that clinicians might consider as a resource. We'll look at how to write an effective nature prescription, and we'll introduce the concept of *therapeutic nature language*. We will review the current research that supports the practice of writing nature prescriptions and offer several examples of nature-based exercises that can be incorporated into a nature prescription.

THE PRACTICE OF WRITING NATURE PRESCRIPTIONS IN PATIENT CARE

Research provides ample evidence that when people live in areas with green space—near local parks and gardens, or have access to a backyard—they gain mental health and physical health benefits. As this evidence becomes more mainstream, there are a growing number of health care initiatives to motivate people to spend time outdoors engaging nature. Encouraging people to spend time in nature is an example of a wider practice of *social prescribing*. Social prescribing connects people to the community resources that address social determinants of health. One environmental determinant of health is access to nature (Tate et al., 2024). The Network for Excellence in Health Innovation estimated that 59% of an individual's health determinants can be positively influenced by nature-based health interventions (Stryer, 2024).

Many chronic illnesses can be associated with the lack of nature connectedness including the psychological conditions of anxiety, depression, and attention deficit disorder, as well as the physiological conditions of diabetes, hypertension, myopia, and obesity. These conditions may be preventable, treatable, and even reversible with an added nature-based approach. Internal medicine physician John La Puma (2023) defines nature-based medicine as the prescriptive, evidence-based use of natural settings and nature-based interventions, with a mission to prevent and treat disease and improve well-being. Though the field of nature-based medicine is just emerging in the United States, it has been taught and practiced in Asia and the EU for decades. Medical schools in Japan, South Korea, Demark, the Netherlands, and the U.K. have all offered medical education in nature-based medicine. In Tokyo's Nippon Medical School, forest therapy—shinrin-yoku—was first identified in 1982 and is now practiced by more than five million people. Prescribing forest bathing has become a cornerstone of preventative health care in Japan. New Zealand physicians have been writing nature-based prescriptions since 1998, Scottish physicians have been authorized to prescribe nature to their patients since 2018, and Canadian physicians have since 2020. Licensed health care providers in four Canadian provinces can now prescribe a free pass to Canada's national parks (Moxley, 2022).

The first U.S. medical school to include nature-based medicine, the Center for Nature and Health, was established in 2016 at UC San Francisco at the UCSF Benioff Children's Hospital. Directed by Nooshin Razani, the center utilizes nature prescriptions with underserved children and their families to combat chronic childhood conditions. The center is involved in ongoing research on the effects of nature prescribing and offers training to physicians and other health care providers in writing nature prescriptions for families.

Another program in the United States that has focused on reconnecting kids and their families to nature is Park Rx America (PRA). Pioneered by Robert Zarr, a pediatrician at Unity Health Care in Washington, DC, PRA is a nonprofit that works with several partner organizations and volunteers to rate parks across the country for their accessibility, cleanliness, level of activity, and safety. Park Rx programs are organized in local communities and reflect the nature experiences available in each community. PRA developed a searchable database by zip code that providers can access to share with their patients or clients (Zarr et al., 2017). The PRA website is a valuable resource for clinicians who want to learn more about incorporating nature prescriptions with local nearby nature and community parks (https://parkrxamerica.org/).

HOW MUCH NATURE DO WE NEED?

As in the medical field, practitioners in the psychological field are recognizing the impact of nature connectedness in the lives of their patients and clients. In Chapter 1 we highlighted some of the studies that demonstrate that increased time spent in the outdoors is associated with mental health benefits including decreased risk of depression, loneliness, and anxiety, and improved sleep, restoration, and a sense of well-being.

The term *nature prescribing* has been applied broadly to any effort by health care professionals to encourage people to spend more time in nature—from counseling about the benefits of nature contact, to writing down specific directions about how much time to spend in local nearby nature, to programming activities with participants in the outdoors (Tate et al., 2024). Not surprisingly, as researchers provide evidence for the efficacy of nature prescribing, the questions of "how much nature do we need" or "what dose of nature is appropriate" inevitably are raised. As environmental determinants of health, these are fair questions. Like other social prescribing recommendations that offer guidelines for how many hours of sleep we need, how many daily servings of fruits and veggies we should eat, and how many steps we should be walking each day, a baseline of time in nature could be a useful guideline. This is especially true in our urbanized, tech-driven culture where more than 50% of us live in cities and North Americans report spending over 90% of their time indoors. Those who work indoors constantly, tethered to their devices and relatively sedentary, are among those most at risk. Our disconnection from the natural world impacts our physical and mental health, so educating clients to the benefits of spending time in the outdoors and discussing how much time to spend outdoors has been shown to be beneficial.

But as a mental health clinician, it is important to remember that ecotherapy expands the clinician's therapeutic focus to include the client's *relationship* with the more-than-human world. By including nature prescriptions in our client care, the clinician encourages *interacting* with the natural world and developing a relationship with it.

The nature prescription gives the client permission to take the time to *be* in nature. Beyond nature exposure, ecotherapy encourages the client to connect with the natural world, to develop a kinship with it, and to feel more fully alive. Studies have shown that direct physical contact with nature produces significantly greater positive affect than virtual exposure to nature such as viewing nature photos or nature videos. A recent study concluded that the quality of the natural setting, not just the quantity of time spent in the setting, is important in generating positive psychological states such as awe, happiness, and joy (Ballew & Omoto, 2018). This is an important consideration for the clinician when writing a nature prescription.

WHAT MAKES AN EFFECTIVE
NATURE PRESCRIPTION

As clinicians expand their scope of treatment to include a client's relationship with the natural world, nature prescriptions provide an avenue to cocreate experiences with the client to engage with nature. The term *nature* here refers to a broad range of natural elements a client might interact with, from tending potted plants on their deck to mindful walks in a local park, to sitting on a beach observing ocean waves, to a hike in a wilderness area. As we will see in the examples that follow, tailoring the written nature prescription to the individual client by utilizing what you learned at the intake session and by including the client in the creation of the prescription ensures greater compliance and can empower the client as an active agent in their care. The goal is to encourage people not only to make more time in their lives for nature, but also to foster a relationship with it. Individuals who are staying healthy by spending time engaged with the outdoors are practicing a form of preventive self-care. Those with mental health symptoms may benefit from spending time engaged with nature as a form of early intervention to lessen the progression and mitigate the impact of their symptoms.

As with other interventions, the clinician must meet the client where they are. The intake questions discussed in the previous chapter offer the clinician insight into the individual's past experience in nature and their current interests, vulnerabilities, activities, and relationship with the natural world. Understanding the client's current access to nature, their openness to engage with nature, and their physical capacity to do so is important.

Unlike a prescription written for a pharmaceutical, where the clinician makes the decision about what substance and in what dose is best and the patient is a passive recipient, when writing a prescription for nature, the clinician invites the client to cocreate the prescription. This ensures that the client is comfortable with the prescribed activity and is on board to make the effort to follow through.

It is important to be as specific as possible when writing a nature prescription—especially for those individuals who may not have a lot of experience in moving out into nature. I learned about the importance of specificity through experience. Early on in my practice of prescribing nature, I made the mistaken assumption that if someone was taking a 20-minute walk in the park, they were noticing the sights, sounds, and smells that surrounded them. When I asked that first client about these sensory experiences, the client just looked at me and had no idea how to reply. She told me she was listening to a favorite artist through her earbuds, and she had taken her dog with her and had let him off leash. She spent part of the walk getting the dog to return to her. I learned that I needed to be very specific in the instructions and consult with the client to be sure they understood and were in agreement.

A general introductory prescription for a 20-minute walk in the park might read like this:

> Take a walk in XYZ Park for a minimum of 20 minutes, three times this week. Be aware of what you see, hear, smell, and feel through your senses. Notice what draws your attention. Notice your breathing. Notice where your thoughts go. Give yourself a few minutes to just be.

A well-written nature prescription will include a specific exercise or activity to happen in a specific place or location for a specified or minimum duration of time for a specified number of times in the week.

This covers the four parts of an effective nature prescription: place, activity, frequency, and duration.

I have found writing down the nature prescription on a prescription pad and giving it to the client encourages follow through and conveys the importance of the activity. I created a simple prescription pad that shows my business logo and contact information and has space for the client's name and the date the prescription was written. Space is provided to handwrite the agreed upon activity with "Rx" at the top of the space, then a place for the provider's signature. Clients seem to appreciate the formality of the written prescription.

The prescription may include additional details depending on the goals for the prescription and feedback from the client in the co-creation process. Self-assessment of symptoms, if any, on a scale of 1–10 before and after the activity can help to evaluate effectiveness. Writing a nature prescription to help the client address a particular issue they face—loss, grief, anger, loneliness, emotional exhaustion, burnout, mild-to-moderate depression, or anxiety—can be a potent therapeutic intervention. Those prescriptions require thoughtful insight and planning on the part of the clinician. The next section introduces the concept of therapeutic nature language. This concept can be helpful as the clinician plans the kind of engagement between the client and nature they wish to write into their nature prescription.

La Puma (2019) reminds clinicians to "walk the talk." The strongest predictor for patient behavior change is their provider's behavior. Clinicians who exercise will encourage their patients to do so more than those who don't exercise, and the same is true for other health-related behaviors like eating a healthy diet, practicing meditation, or getting outdoors into nature regularly. Practicing healthy behaviors ourselves leads to greater counseling of others in this area. If the clinician schedules time to walk outdoors, they can mention it to clients in their discussions.

Introducing Therapeutic Nature Language

Nature language is a concept that provides a narrative to speak about biophilic interactions, the meaning associated with these interactions between humans and nonhuman nature, and the emotional responses they engender (Hasbach, 2015; Kahn et al., 2012). This concept can aid clinicians in writing effective nature prescriptions.

Nature language is composed of *interaction patterns* that represent fundamental ways we interact with elements of nature that engender meaningful human experience. Many interaction patterns developed during our species' evolutionary history as we evolved embedded in the natural world, and they can be thought of as primal (original) interactions humans have with other elements of nature. Examples of primal interaction patterns include: *sitting by fire, sleeping under the night sky, building a shelter,* and *cooking around the fire circle.* Interaction patterns can be experienced on a continuum of wild experiences to more domestic ones. A wilder manifestation of the interaction pattern *sitting by fire* might be experienced by sitting around a campfire under the night sky alone or with others. A more domestic version of that same interaction pattern might entail sitting on the porch by a propane fire pit or sitting by the gas fireplace in one's family room.

Nature language provides a systematic way of thinking about what elements of nature or what experiences in nature might be most potent for a therapeutic nature prescription. The clinician can incorporate nature language into the therapeutic process by listening deeply for interaction patterns in the client's stories and creating opportunities for encounters between the client and nature that deeply *touch on* or *attend to* an issue on which they are working. For example, I worked with a client who was trying to close the chapter on a long-term relationship, but kept in her words "going back" to the relationship that she knew was not good for her. From earlier sessions, I understood that she was an avid photographer and traveler. She was planning a trip to the mountains where she anticipated beautiful views and was looking forward to photographing the rugged landscape. I asked her if she would be willing to take photos of the mountains at sunset. I also asked her to journal about the experience of the sunset and reflect on any parallels she felt about the closing of that chapter in her life. When she came back into the office, she brought a few photos of the sunset to show me, and she shared some of her journaling notes. What struck her was that once the sun was going down below the horizon, it didn't turn back. It had its own beauty as it disappeared behind the mountains, and there was a stunning afterglow in the evening sky. She related feeling a sense of freedom as she thought of the afterglow, and said for her it signified that life would go on with its own beauty.

In this example, focusing on a transitional time in nature—the sunset—I incorporated the interaction pattern *interacting with the periodicity of nature*. This nature prescription invited the client to reflect on her own life transition in the larger context of the transitional time of the day in nature. We will take a deeper dive into therapeutic nature language in the next chapter.

Nature-Based Exercises to Incorporate Into Nature Prescriptions

In this section, I have included a few exercises that can be tailored to a client's specific situation and needs. The exercises offer the clinician some suggestions to consider for use in writing their nature prescriptions.

Special Place Prescription. With the goal of encouraging the individual to form a relationship with the larger natural world, I have found this exercise to be effective for clients and instructive for my graduate students. Clients select a special place that they agree to visit for 1 month. They are asked to go to the same spot two to three times per week, at various times of the day and in various weather conditions. We discuss how long they can spend at their chosen location— usually between 15 minutes to a half hour. At the beginning of the month-long prescription, I ask them to focus on these questions:

1. How do you feel in this place, and what state of mind arises?
2. What drew you to this place?
3. What relationships do you recognize in this place?
4. What physical sensations and sensory awarenesses do you notice when you are here?
5. What are you curious about regarding this place?

This exercise fosters a gradual deepening of relationship with a particular place through heightened sensory perception, expanded knowledge, and a familiarity over time.

The Contemplative Nature Walk. The contemplative nature walk is a nature prescription exercise that asks the client to spend a couple of hours slowly walking through a safe natural location that they have identified and ponder the concerns that have brought them into therapy. We talk about how the walk will have a ritualized beginning, middle, and end. It gives the individual permission to slow their pace, carve out some time in a busy schedule, unplug from technology, and walk with (or sit with) their concerns. Clients often bring back a found object that drew their attention and held some meaning for them as they spent time with their thoughts.

Screen-Time and Nature-Time Log. During the last decade people have been spending more time engaged with technology and less time engaged with the outdoors. As mentioned earlier, in 2019 the average adult in the U.S. reported spending 11.5 hours each day consuming media, while half of 18–29 year olds said they were online "almost constantly." That same year, Bratman and colleagues (2019) at Stanford University showed that a 45-minute walk in nearby nature can improve mood, creativity, and working memory.

To raise awareness of a client's screen time and nature time, I ask them to keep a log for 7 consecutive days. For the screen-time log, they are asked to record the date, the type of digital technology they are interacting with (e.g., computer, cell phone, tablet, TV), the activity (e.g., work, school, entertainment, communication with friends and family, gaming), and the amount of time spent with the screen. For the same time period, I ask them to record the time spent outdoors interacting with nature, noting the date, location, activity, and the amount of time spent.

To complete the exercise, I ask them to analyze their screen-time and nature-time logs, without self-judgment. What do they notice? What are they happy with? What would they like to modify?

Looking for Nature's Patterns. To get a client to take notice of the beauty of the natural world around them, this exercise can be very useful and nonthreatening because they can do it in and around their home. As a species, humans are attracted to beauty in nature that is rich in detail and diversity while simultaneously ordered and organized. This quality of organized complexity is known as fractal geometry. Fractals are patterns found in nature where the parts reflect the whole. The basic patterns are similar to one another, but not identical. Examples of fractal patterns in nature include snowflakes, veins in leaves of a tree, the fiddleheads of a fern, river deltas, ocean wave marks in the sand, and the spiral of a shell. Architectural features such as stained-glass windows and designs for fabrics and wallpaper often incorporate fractal patterns.

I ask clients to look around their home and see if they can identify natural or human-made objects that include fractal patterns. If they are open to it, they may be asked to draw the fractal pattern that they found. This exercise heightens awareness of how we are surrounded by the detailed beauty of nature.

The 24/7 Nature Challenge. This exercise asks the individual to spend a minimum of 24 minutes outdoors in nature each day for 7 consecutive days. Suggestions for what to do can be included. Modeled after the David Suzuki Foundation 30x30 Nature Challenge, a global initiative introduced in 2012 to encourage people to get outdoors for a minimum of 30 minutes per day for 30 days, this pared-back version is a good way to introduce a behavior change to someone who does not get outdoors on a regular basis. It can be a good follow-up to a discussion of the benefits of nature contact on our physical and psychological health and well-being.

CONCLUDING THOUGHTS ON
NATURE PRESCRIPTIONS

Our species came of age in a world far wilder than the one we live in today. Much of that wildness still resides within us and needs to be rediscovered, reengaged, and reintegrated into our lives for us to flourish (Hasbach, 2015; Kahn & Hasbach, 2013). But most traditional therapy stops at the urban boundary and takes place in an indoor office space with a focus almost exclusively on human-to-human interactions. Many of the nature-based practices and methods of ecotherapy invite direct experience with nature that affords heightened sensorial experiences and perceptions that connect our inner world and the outer landscape. The skillful ecotherapist recognizes the subtle and often impactful influence of nature on the therapeutic work. Nature prescriptions can deepen clients' therapeutic experience and foster a greater awareness of their interconnection with the natural world. Nature prescriptions can encourage clients to take time for quiet and solitude, allowing their thoughts and feelings to become more embodied. And nature prescriptions provide rich images, metaphors, and direct experiences to work with in subsequent sessions.

When we refer to nature prescriptions, some people in the field are concerned with the medicalization of nature. They raise the important point that as ecotherapists, we don't want to support merely using nature for our health benefit. They are voicing a sensitivity that those of us who deeply care about the natural world have, and we don't want to foster seeing nature only as a resource for our use. But I wonder if we can reframe the practice of writing nature prescriptions—or moving outdoors for therapy for that matter—as the naturalization of medicine. Ecotherapy practices and nature-based medicine recognize that we are part of nature. We *are* nature! We need interactions and engagement with our kith-and-kin to be fully human and to thrive. When we encourage clients to interact with elements of nature, we offer them an opportunity to approach their concerns and issues from a holistic perspective—considering their sensorial embodied selves, in addition to the cognitive self we typically work with. We invite the client to step outdoors and experience the world around them in real time and in the first person, rather than seeing the world mediated by a two-dimensional screen. When this happens, it offers the opportunity to not only form a relationship with nature, but to fall in love with it, to care for it, and to protect it.

Baba Diom, a forest engineer from Senegal, wisely stated in a paper he presented in 1968 in New Delhi at the General Assembly of the International Union for the Conservation of Nature and Natural Resources (IUCN):

> In the end, we will conserve only what we love,
> We will love only what we understand,
> And we will understand only what we are taught.

8

THERAPEUTIC NATURE
LANGUAGE, RITUALS,
AND METAPHORS

The previous two chapters focused on nature-based methods of moving the therapy session outdoors and writing nature prescriptions. We introduced the concept of therapeutic nature language and discussed making use of nature metaphor and imagery in practice. This chapter takes a deeper dive into understanding therapeutic nature language and how the clinician might use it to enrich their nature prescriptions, guided meditations, therapeutic dialogue, and nature engagement. We'll also look at the historical usage of ritual and ceremony in healing and consider how outdoor rituals can be powerful when cocreated by the therapist and client. Finally, we'll revisit the earlier discussion on metaphors and consider how they might be useful in formulating nature prescriptions and outdoor experiences.

To begin thinking about these concepts and practices, I would like the reader to take a moment to think about an experience you've had in nature that was particularly memorable. Write a paragraph or two about that experience. With what form(s) of nature were you engaged? Where did the experience take place? What were you doing? What made the experience memorable? What feelings do you recall associated with the experience? Be as descriptive as possible. Note what feelings come up for you now as you recall this experience in nature.

INCORPORATING THERAPEUTIC NATURE
LANGUAGE INTO THERAPY

From the beginning, our species has been intimately embedded in the natural world. We co-evolved and interacted with elements of nature and with other nonhuman beings. Much of our primal wisdom and deep knowing that allowed for our species' survival is within each of us (Kahn & Hasbach, 2013). But in recent decades, we find ourselves increasingly removed from the natural world and interacting with it less and less. Robert Michael Pyle (1993) coined the term, "the extinction of experience" to describe this ongoing alienation of humans from the rest of nature. Pyle emphasized that direct experience with the natural environment is vital to developing an emotional intimacy with it.

In a chapter titled, "Building the Science Base: Ecopsychology Meets Clinical Epidemiology," Howard Frumkin (2012), former dean of the School of Public Health and professor emeritus at the University of Washington, carefully reviewed an extensive body of empirical literature that covered the physical and psychological effects of interacting with animals and plants, connecting with natural landscapes, and engaging in wilderness experiences. He concluded that there is ample evidence that interactions with nature are *essential* for our physical and psychological well-being.

Think about what implications biophilic interactions might have for health care and education, for therapy and the built environment. How can we bring more nature—more wild nature—into our work and into our individual lives? Here we look at how we can utilize the concept of nature language to deepen our engagement with nature—to rewild therapy—so that we might enrich and enliven our work with clients and patients.

Earlier, we defined nature language as a concept that provides a way to speak about biophilic interactions between humans and nonhuman nature, the meaning associated with these interactions, and the emotional responses they engender. The concept is grounded in the belief that for humans to thrive—for us to be fully human—we must be *in relationship* with the natural world of which we are a part. As Kellert (2012) eloquently stated,

> We will never be truly healthy, satisfied, or fulfilled if we live apart and alienated from the environment from which we evolved. Much of what we value and cherish as distinctively human—our capacity to care, reason, love, create, find beauty, and know happiness—continues to be contingent on our diverse ties to nature. (p. x)

The concept of nature language can be compared to a similar endeavor in conservation biology. Conservation biologists believe that we cannot save what we do not know. They work to discover, name, and classify biological species and the ways in which species interact. Similarly, nature language attempts to identify and classify the diverse and meaningful ways that people interact with nature (Kahn et al., 2012). But as we spend more time indoors and less time interacting with nature, we lose the language to speak of those interactions.

In the introduction to the book *Home Ground: Language for an American Landscape*, the renowned nature writer Barry Lopez writes that it is a common observation about American culture that we are groping for a renewed sense of place and community. He wonders whether the accelerated demands of daily life in our modern culture indirectly undermine something foundational and essential in our lives—a deep sense of knowing a place along with a sense of affirmation with our neighbors that the place we've chosen is beautiful, profound, and worthy of our lives—that contributes to a deep sense of belonging that comes with knowing a place intimately (Lopez & Gwartney, 2006). That volume focuses on the language that we have lost to precisely describe and know a landscape and the various nature elements and features that are part of it. Nature language focuses on the interactions: what we do in a place or with an element of nature. The intention of the concept of nature language is to be mindful of our human–nature interactions, value these interactions and prioritize them in our lives, and protect the nature that makes them possible.

Nature language provides a conceptual framework that is proving to be valuable in a variety of settings including: (1) tech-focused companies that are looking to encourage creativity in employees by capitalizing on the restorative benefits of direct contact with nature through the design of the work environment including the outdoors, (2) land-use planning firms that are focused on addressing specific desires of community stakeholders while prioritizing natural features of the landscape, (3) schools that are moving their classrooms outdoors to enhance place-based, experiential education, and (4) health care providers and psychotherapists looking to incorporate nature-based methods into their therapeutic work with patients and clients. Here we focus on the latter application.

Nature language is comprised of interaction patterns—an interaction between humans and some element of nonhuman nature—that can be manifest in an endless number of ways in wild or in more domestic settings. For example, *sitting by fire, building a shelter, sleeping under the night sky, moving away from settlement and return, interacting with the periodicity of nature, foraging, walking nature's edges, being by water,* and *recognizing and being recognized by nonhuman nature.* Interaction patterns such as these are often experienced in combination with one another and are often experienced on a continuum of wild manifestations to more domestic ones (Kahn et al., 2012). Interaction patterns emerge depending on the affordances of the landscapes involved and the person interacting with the environment.

When I am teaching graduate counseling students about this concept of nature language, I ask them to write about an experience they've had in nature that was memorable and deeply meaningful to them. Students are then asked to share their stories in dyads. While one student describes their experience, the other student listens for:

1. What *element(s) of nature* was involved?
2. What *action(s)* was involved? What was the person doing? What senses were activated?
3. What *psychological experiences* were described? What made the experience meaningful?

The listener is instructed to notice what nature nouns are used, what verbs are used to describe actions, what sensorial descriptors are noted, and what adjectives or adverbs they hear. This is a way to learn to listen for interaction patterns.

Therapeutic nature language provides a narrative to discuss the biophilic interactions that we as clinicians want to foster in the ecotherapeutic process. It helps us think about what patterns of interactions between the client and nature could serve to deepen the therapeutic work—to rewild the process of therapy—to allow nature itself to be the primary therapist or guide.

In the previous chapter, I shared an example of how I utilized therapeutic nature language in writing a nature prescription for a client who was trying to close the chapter on a long-term relationship but kept going back to the relationship. She was traveling to the mountains and expressed her willingness to take photos of the sunset and journal about the experience of the sunset and reflect on any parallels she felt about closing that chapter in her life. The therapeutic nature language interaction patterns that were engaged in this prescription included *moving away from settlement and returning* (in this case, traveling to the mountains), and *interacting with the periodicity of nature* (the sunset).

In another case, the client was a 17-year-old boy whose parents had separated and become embroiled in a bitter divorce. He had little structure in his life, was truant and failing his senior year of high school, and was living between his parents' homes. His father brought him to see me after he had been pulled over by the police for speeding and broke down crying to the officer and saying he wanted to kill himself. Fortunately, the police officer took him to the emergency room and contacted his father. At the time of our first session, the boy showed little affect and described "feeling numb." He was apathetic to failing his senior year and his parents' inevitable divorce. In that first session, I learned that he had loved to go fishing when he was younger. During one of our early sessions, I suggested we meet at the fishing spot he mentioned and I said he was welcome to bring his fishing rod. While we sat by the water's edge, he began to talk about how his dad had taught him to fish on that very river. Partway through the session, I suggested that he dangle his feet in the water and I did the same. The clear water was icy cold. He began to share his feelings of anger, sadness, and feeling "out of control of so much of his life." It was as though the icy water woke up his feelings and allowed them to be released. We talked about feeling alive, a sense of belonging, and the consistency that place had been in his life. The themes of belonging and attachment were central to our therapeutic work. The therapeutic nature language interaction patterns included *moving away from settlement and return, sitting at the water's edge, immersion in water,* and *fishing.*

Look at the paragraph you wrote at the beginning of this chapter about a meaningful interaction you had with nature. Try to identify what interaction patterns were involved. Reread what you wrote and describe what you were doing using a verb; add a preposition and a nature noun. See if you can envision different examples of this same interaction pattern. Coming upon a wild animal while on a hike may be a very memorable experience. The bear sees me and I see the bear. Our eyes meet. The interaction pattern has been named *recognizing and being recognized by nonhuman other.* This interaction pattern can be enacted in many different environments and with different forms of nonhuman Other. I see the deer in my backyard and the deer sees me. A more domestic version of this same pattern is being greeted by the family dog when you get home.

By incorporating therapeutic nature language into therapy through intentionally working with interaction patterns and their varied manifestations, we can speak more systematically about behaviors that we engage in with nature and address the emotions and psychological experiences that result. In so doing, we create opportunities for clients to reawaken deeper, authentic feelings of connection and belonging in the natural world.

By 2050, it is estimated that 70% of the world's population will be living in urban settings. As so many of us find ourselves living farther removed from nature, we must examine how to stay *in relationship* with the more-than-human world in order to flourish as individuals and as a species. By recognizing interaction patterns that are deeply embedded in our evolutionary development, therapeutic nature language can be utilized to articulate ways to intentionally and mindfully reconnect ourselves to the human–nature relationship through direct experience. By incorporating the concept of nature language into our work, we can bring more nature—more wild nature—into the lives of our clients, as well as our own.

Cocreating Rituals With Your Clients

Rituals and ceremony have played an important role in healing for most of recorded history. Our ancestors lived close to the natural world and depended on it for their physical, social, and spiritual life. Rituals provided a sense of order and security and a sense of control over life's uncertainties. Rituals also helped people move from one social stage of life to another. From today's modern, urban, technological perspective, the notion of ritual may not seem particularly relevant. But we deal with many of the same universal issues as our ancestors: fears of uncertainty, the unknown, and the uncontrollable.

The *Cambridge Dictionary* defines ritual as "a set of actions or words performed in a regular way, often as part of a religious ceremony. A ritual is also any act done regularly, usually without thinking about it: My morning ritual includes reading the newspaper while I drink my coffee."

As a clinician, I have found that the word ritual can be tricky in therapy. The word holds various connotations for people, so it is important to understand the client's perspective of it. Other references to ritual include ceremony and even being mindful as one approaches a defined activity.

The natural world provides many opportunities for including rituals in therapeutic work. In the outdoors, we are surrounded by signs of change and cycles of life that are rich in metaphors. Rituals can be designed to acknowledge a rite of passage or mark a life transition. Rituals can facilitate letting go of a painful event or acknowledging a loss. They can celebrate an important accomplishment, mark a joyous life event, or facilitate renewal, reconnection, or resilience. The natural world is filled with metaphors that can be incorporated into rituals that help us see our own growth and healing.

Depth psychologist Bill Plotkin (2003) suggests that rituals can open us to transpersonal experiences, alter consciousness, facilitate communion with the Other, and help us see ourselves and the world from a perspective more resonant with soul.

In the context of this book, rituals are useful in therapeutic practice to mark transformations rather than thinking that the ritual creates or is responsible for the transformation. Rituals should not be performed or prescribed that are beyond the therapist's scope of training. Likewise, the therapist should be sensitive to the client's potential preconceived ideas about rituals, and the creation of rituals should include the client in the cocreative process.

One of the most powerful examples of making use of ritual in outdoor therapy comes from Ira Orchin (2004), who wrote about his work with a client, Sam, whose son was a New York City police officer who was killed in the September 11, 2001 attack on New York's Twin Towers. Orchin recalls that after working through the client's grief, they created a ritual for Sam to say good-bye to his son and move forward with his life. He recalled that he and Sam gathered wood and built a fire at the edge of a lake. As they watched the flames and the setting sun, Sam shared stories about his son and read the transcripts of his son's final phone call, which the NYPD had given him. When he finished reading, he wept, then crumpled the pages of the transcript and burned them. He sang a farewell song and hurled several pieces of burning wood into the water. Sam then had an imaginary conversation with his son, who told him, "Sometimes you must go into a burning building" (p. 2). Orchin noted that the power of this ritual came from the elements of nature: the fire, the water, the setting sun, and the openness of space. I ask the reader to think about the therapeutic nature language interaction patterns involved in this ritual: *sitting by water, building a fire, sitting around fire, moving away from settlement and return, interacting with the periodicity of nature.*

When I cocreate a ritual with a client as part of their nature prescription, I draw on the vision-quest work of Steven Foster and Meredith Little (1997). They discuss a series of activities that helps move clients into a natural setting mindfully, with openness and receptivity. First, the client prepares for the experience by setting a clear intention. Second, they cross a threshold by walking over a line on the ground such as stepping over a stick or walking through a natural portal. A marker like this creates a container by defining the boundary of special time and special place. Then they experience the ritual that they've created. Next, they cross back over the threshold and close the container upon their return. Finally, they return with gifts to integrate into their lives (Hasbach, 2012).

During the planning phase of ritual creation, I give the client a handout that provides some general guidelines to help them create their personal ritual. The handout includes these points:

1. *Decide in advance if you will enact the ritual alone or if you will invite others to join you.* As you plan your ritual, allow space for spontaneity. Not knowing what will unfold in the ritual space is part of the power of ritual.

2. *Set your intention for the ritual.* The ritual space can offer a safe zone to release some aspect of yourself that may be hindering your fullness and growth. It may offer the opportunity to claim some aspect of yourself that has been silenced. Take the time to fully develop your intention for the ritual.

3. *Create the ritual space.* You may choose to perform the ritual in a place that holds special meaning for you or in a place that feels physically and emotionally safe. Gather the objects that will help you deepen the ritual experience: meaningful objects, things that are remembrances of your ancestors, photos, natural objects, flowers, candles, or incense. Many cultures incorporate the four elements of earth, fire, water, and air into their rituals.

4. *Mark the beginning of the ritual.* To symbolically mark the beginning of a ritual, you may consider lighting a candle or ceremonial fire. You may choose to meditate or begin with a prayer, a chant, or a moment of silence.

5. *Perform the ritual.* Think about what you can do to enact your stated intention. Be creative. You may consider:
   a. Speaking aloud, allowing nature (and perhaps invited humans) to witness for you

    b. Recording the experience in your journal

    c. Writing what you are releasing on a piece of paper or
a twig or popsicle stick and burning it or burying it

    d. Writing the burdens you are carrying onto stones and
tossing them into the water

    e. Celebrating an accomplishment by creating a piece of
nature art to take home

    f. Celebrating a new beginning by planting a tree

6. *Mark the end of the ritual.* Just as you marked the beginning of your ritual space, you will want to close the ritual space. If others have joined you, you might consider a celebration with food and drink.

A few years ago, I worked with Jesse, an intelligent, successful woman in her mid-30s. Jesse carried a great deal of mistrust and unfinished anger about a relationship in which she was betrayed and deeply hurt. She avoided risking another relationship for 6 years and buried herself in her work, building a successful business. But she felt unfulfilled and wished to release the anger, hurt, and fear that held her back from considering another relationship. After several months of working together, I asked her what she felt ready to let go of. We discussed the power of ritual as the opportunity to not just talk about letting go of the anger and resentment and fear, but to enact letting go of those emotions. Jesse gathered several small twigs and sticks and wrote the thoughts and fears she felt ready to release—one on each stick. She invited a close friend to accompany her. She built a small fire in her backyard firepit and ceremonially burned each stick after she read aloud what she was ready to release. Her ritual was witnessed by her friend, the nature in her backyard, and the night sky.

Rituals help us create sacred space and set an intention to be open to other ways of knowing that have long been with us as humans. In cocreating rituals with clients, the clinician can think about the elements of nature, the interaction patterns, and the potential metaphors that will make the enactment of the ritual deeply meaningful for their client.

Making Use of Nature Metaphors

In Chapter 6 we introduced nature metaphors and offered a brief description of how they enrich nature-based therapy. We defined metaphors as a tool for the transfer of meaning from something that is known or easily recognized to something that is new or more challenging to articulate. We saw how items in the nature basket can provide powerful prompts for clients to talk about feelings and how they can be descriptors of the client's inner experiences. Clinicians practicing ecotherapy listen for nature metaphors during the intake session, during therapeutic dialogue, and while clients share their experience of a nature prescription. Research findings show that metaphors occur at a higher rate when describing emotions and discussing emotional experiences, making metaphors even more important for therapists to recognize and address (Wagener, 2017).

Metaphors can be client-generated or therapist-generated. Client-generated metaphors can help the clinician understand how the client is conceptualizing their experience and can be useful to facilitate insight and move the therapeutic process forward. The therapist asks the client to elaborate on the metaphor and follows up by asking questions to provide more detail including the emotions associated with the metaphor. Following the client's elaboration, additional questions and reflections from the therapist support the generation of client insight. The client may say "I'm caught in a whirlwind." The therapist might ask, "Can you tell me more about your experience of the whirlwind?" Depending on the client's response, the therapist may ask about the emotions associated with that experience.

Clinician-generated metaphors involve the use of metaphors to intentionally support the therapeutic process. It might involve the reintroduction of metaphors first generated by the client but with changes to support growth or the sharing of new metaphors in a way to help the client recognize thoughts, feelings, and behaviors (Wagener, 2017). In the example in Chapter 7 of the client who was asked to take photos of the sunset and journal about her thoughts related to the closing of the relationship, the metaphor of the setting sun and its disappearance below the horizon helped the client to embody her feelings related to "not going back" and to recognize there was a beauty to life in marking the end of that day (or chapter in her life).

Another approach to therapist-introduced metaphors is the *disquisition*, a narrative form of metaphor that involves telling a story that involves similar interactions and concerns as those of the client. These stories may be fictional stories or fairytale stories that are closely related to the client's issues. The purpose of the stories is to normalize the client's experience, increase insight, and facilitate new perspectives (Millikin & Johnson, 2000). With a client who was a student of environmental science and who was working on climate change science specifically, I chose to tell the parable of the hummingbird to help him deal with the overwhelm he was experiencing. The client wondered how he would be able to do the hard work of being on the frontlines of climate change science without burning out or losing hope. In the parable of the hummingbird, the forest is ablaze and all the animals are escaping across the river to avoid the fire. The story chronicles the harrowing escape of many of the animals as their forest home burns. There is great sadness and exhaustion and fear expressed as they talk with one another. They then notice the tiny hummingbird dip down to the river and fly toward the burning forest. The hummingbird does this again and again until it must land on the far shore to rest. The other animals ask the hummingbird "What are you thinking? You could have been killed. What are you doing?" and the hummingbird replies "All that I can." My client was tearful as this story was told and he was able to elaborate on his own experience and feeling of doing all that he can in the hard work of addressing climate change.

CONCLUSION

Therapeutic nature language, rituals, and metaphors are all tools to deepen the work we do with our clients and patients. These tools enhance nature-based methods that move us beyond the cognitive skills we are taught in our training. All of these tools require thoughtful, careful applications and put the burden of responsibility on the clinician to be trained and competent in their use. The next chapter focuses on ethical responsibilities the ecotherapist must consider.

PART III

Practical Considerations

9

ETHICAL CONSIDERATIONS, FORMS OF ECOTHERAPY, AND SPECIAL POPULATIONS

We have seen that the nature-based practices of moving therapy sessions outdoors and writing nature prescriptions offer an abundance of benefits to the therapeutic process. These practices also create unique challenges the clinician must consider. This chapter revisits some of the issues raised in Chapter 6 related to the logistical challenges and the potential barriers to moving therapy sessions outdoors. We then look at three areas of ethical concern when moving therapy out of the four walls of the office setting—confidentiality, avoiding harm, and competency. We'll see what various professional organizations' codes of ethics offer as guidelines on these important topics. Then we'll turn our attention to the various forms ecotherapy can take and discuss special populations that especially benefit from nature-based practices.

LOGISTICAL CHALLENGES

In Chapter 6, I highlighted several logistic challenges that must be considered such as scheduling concerns when meeting outside the office setting, the location of the office and its proximity to a natural space that works for therapy, and unpredictable weather conditions. I also discussed topics that should be considered as the clinician prepares to move therapy sessions outdoors: assessing the client's appropriateness for outdoor therapy, their comfort level with the outdoors, their physical capacities, and safety issues. Other topics to discuss with clients include options for how to handle confidentiality issues when outdoors, health concerns that might be exacerbated by the environment, and any cultural norms, trauma, or personal history with the outdoors to which the clinician should be sensitive.

I reviewed the importance of documenting the preparation discussion in the client's chart. This is especially important if you are moving the sessions to wilder environments where there may be more unpredictability and greater risks involved.

Limitations set by agency or organizational rules and policies, especially as they relate to minors and other vulnerable populations, must also be considered.

ETHICAL CONSIDERATIONS

From my years of practice and from discussions with colleagues who incorporate nature-based practices into their work, I see three areas of ethical concerns that the clinician must address when moving therapy sessions outdoors: confidentiality, avoiding harm, and competency. These three areas are discussed in the existing codes of ethics held by the American Psychological Association (APA, 2017), the American Counseling Association (ACA, 2014), and the National Association of Social Workers (NASW, 2021). I assume the European counterparts to these professional groups uphold similar standards. My familiarity is with these U.S. associations; therefore, I will reference them as I discuss how these ethical areas apply to the practice of ecotherapy.

Confidentiality

During the preparation discussion with clients, the clinician should raise the issue of confidentiality with clients and understand how they want to handle certain situations that may arise. For instance, how would they like to handle the situation if we encounter a familiar person while outdoors? We discuss the options and document our conclusions. I also raise the question of how we will manage discussing sensitive material if someone approaches or passes us on the path or trail. In most cases, we simply pause the discussion or lower our voices. There are also times we might choose to find a quiet spot to sit down—an advantage of knowing the environment and convenient stopping points that offer more privacy. It is the clinician's responsibility to raise these potential situations and to support the client in making an informed decision.

The APA Code of Ethics addresses the issue of confidentiality and directs psychologists to discuss the limitations of confidentiality with their clients/patients (4.02, Discussing the Limits of Confidentiality). In part, various sections of the code direct psychologists to take reasonable precautions to protect confidential information, discuss the relevant limits of confidentiality, and direct providers to discuss confidentiality at the outset of the therapeutic relationship and as new circumstances warrant (APA Ethical Principles of Psychologists and Code of Conduct, 2017).

The ACA Code of Ethics is particularly relevant for ecotherapists as it addresses the issue of confidentiality when leaving the confines of the clinical office, indicating that practitioners should consider situations where confidentiality might be breached (ACA, 2014 Code of Ethics).

Avoiding Harm

Most codes of ethics require that clinicians avoid harm to their clients or patients. When clinicians meet with clients in the office, they intentionally work to provide a safe psychological space, and they generally intend to provide a safe physical space for them as well. We assume that our office spaces, health clinics, agency settings, and schools provide a reasonably safe environment for our clients and ourselves. But when we move therapy outdoors, we must do so mindfully and ask what might pose some danger to clients and raise those concerns with them before leaving the office. Safety concerns may be relatively minor in a nearby park or walking path or garden, but when therapy moves to wilder environments like moving water or a mountain trail, clinicians must be prepared and raise the safety concerns with their clients.

The APA Code of Ethics (3.04, Avoiding Harm) directs psychologists to take reasonable steps to avoid harming their clients and to minimize harm where it is foreseeable and unavoidable (APA Ethical Principles of Psychologists and Code of Conduct, 2017).

The ACA Code of Ethics (A.4.a., Avoiding Harm) addresses this issue similarly by directing counselors to avoid harming clients and to minimize or remedy unavoidable or unanticipated harm (ACA Code of Ethics, 2014).

Competency

As the field of ecopsychology continues to develop, and interest in the practice of ecotherapy expands, there are more opportunities for practitioners to acquire relevant training through professional development workshops, conferences, and graduate programs. There are several professional journals publishing relevant research the clinician should be acquainted with, and a substantial body of literature addresses the evolving theories of the human–nature relationship and various practices of ecotherapy. Clinicians need to recognize their limits of competence related to the therapeutic issues of this emerging field.

Similarly, the practitioner needs to be clear about their level of competence related to the outdoor environment where they are conducting their work. It is incumbent upon the practitioner to assess the level of risk involved in a given environment and determine the client's level of competence and confidence to handle the environment. If the therapeutic environment is in an urban park or trail or some other domestic setting, the relative risk may be low. But if therapy moves to wilder environs, the clinician must be clear about their own competence and thoughtfully assess the client's level of ability and comfort. Ultimately, it is the clinician's responsibility to ensure that they are competent and prepared for the environment into which they are taking clients.

The APA Code of Ethics (2.01, Boundaries of Competence) directs psychologists to offer services only within the boundaries of their competence based on their education and training. It further states that in emerging areas of practice in which generally recognized standards of preparatory training don't exist, the psychologist should take reasonable steps to ensure the competence of their work and to protect their clients/patients from harm (APA Ethical Principles of Psychologists and Code of Conduct, 2017).

The ACA Code of Ethics (C.2.a, Boundaries of Competence) directs counselors to practice only within the boundaries of their competence based on their education, training, supervised experience, professional credentials, and appropriate professional experience. The code also addresses new specialty areas of practice by directing counselors to practice in specialty areas new to them only after appropriate education, training, and supervised experience. It goes on to say that while developing skills in new specialty areas, counselors should take steps to ensure the competence of their work and protect others from possible harm (ACA Code of Ethics, 2014).

The National Association of Social Workers Code of Ethics uphold similar standards to those mentioned above.

Our Ethical Responsibility to Nature

There is one area of ethical responsibility that clinicians must consider that is not written in our professional organizations' codes of ethics. That is, as we include the natural world as a partner in the therapeutic process, we have an obligation to recognize not only nature's therapeutic value, but nature's intrinsic value as well. This means interacting with nonhuman nature and natural systems not just as objects or resources to be utilized, but as subjects of a relationship of mutuality and care. Like all relationships, the human–nature relationship involves reciprocity and challenges us to consider our ethical responsibility to the natural world in which we work and of which we are a part.

VARIOUS FORMS OF NATURE-BASED THERAPY

This book focuses primarily on nature-based practices of ecotherapy that the private practice clinician or mental health provider can offer to individuals and couples. In this section we explore other forms of nature-based therapy that include animal-assisted therapy; green space interventions such as horticulture therapy and therapeutic gardening, care farms, forest bathing (shinrin-yoku); and group therapies in wilder environments such as wilderness therapy and adventure therapy.

Animal-Assisted Therapy

Animal-assisted therapy is a form of ecotherapy that incorporates animals—usually dogs, horses, or cats—into the therapeutic process. The clinician, client, and animal work together in therapeutic activities to address treatment goals. Animal-assisted therapy has proven effective in working to address stress, anxiety, depression, autism, ADHD, loneliness, dementia in older adults, emotional and behavioral issues in children, and some medical conditions including coronary heart disease and pain management.

A 1980 study by Erica Friedmann found that patients discharged from a coronary care unit who owned a dog or cat were more likely to survive at a 1-year follow up than the non–pet owner patients. Since then, researchers have offered these explanations for that finding: Interactions with dogs and cats may reduce their human's stress and anxiety, lower heart rate and blood pressure, and invite social interactions with other people addressing loneliness. In 2013, the American Heart Association released a scientific statement saying that pet ownership, especially having a dog, was associated with a lower risk of heart disease. Though most studies are correlational, these potential benefits have spawned numerous programs that focus on pet owners who are older or have disabilities.

Similarly, animal-assisted programs have shown benefits for prison inmates, at-risk youth, students with reading and speech difficulties, and trauma survivors. Reading-to-a-dog programs are now in hundreds of libraries and schools around the United States and abroad. Research suggests that reading aloud in the presence of a dog creates a nonjudgmental environment that allows the child to relax and stay on task. Therapy dogs have also been invaluable in the aftermath of school shootings. Comfort dogs have been part of the trauma team that served to aid children, parents, and first responders with the stress, anxiety, fear, and trauma they suffered.

Some private practice clinicians include a therapy dog in their office practice. Therapy dogs can help to reduce stress and anxiety, improve the client's mood, build rapport between the client and the therapist, enhance the client's social skills, and lower client resistance to therapy. Little is written about how the presence of a therapy dog enhances the work environment for the clinician, but anecdotal evidence suggests that the clinician–therapy dog partnership is a positive one.

Equine-assisted therapy refers to therapeutic activities with horses. Equine therapy has been used to treat anxiety, autism, ADHD, depression, addiction, PTSD, and other mental health disorders in adults and children. During an equine therapy session, the client takes care of the horse with help and direction from the equine therapist or specialist including grooming the animal, feeding it, and leading it around an enclosure. Riding the horse is usually not a component of mental health treatment, but it may occur as part of physical therapy or occupational therapy. After the activity, the client and the therapist process what occurred, what was learned, and what emotions and insights emerged.

Equine therapy is effective, in part, due to the mirroring effect that happens during interactions between the horse and the client. Horses are especially attuned to human emotions and nonverbal signals, and they respond accordingly. A client who is angry or anxious may see the horse pull away or respond negatively. The mirroring process helps the client identify what they are feeling and work to modify their emotions, all in a nonjudgmental environment. Horses are large, powerful creatures and may be intimidating to some people. Engaging with them in a supervised environment can help anxious clients face their fears, practice vulnerability, and build self-esteem. Over time, clients form a bond with their horse that can foster empathy and build trust. Anecdotal evidence suggests that many clients find the practice beneficial, but more research is needed to determine equine therapy's efficacy for specific mental health conditions.

Horticulture Therapy

Horticulture therapy is a green space intervention that involves incorporating gardening and other nature-based activities that is used in rehabilitative, vocational, and community settings. Horticulture therapists have knowledge in plant science, horticultural therapy principles, and horticultural therapy practices. The American Horticultural Therapy Association (AHTA) supports the professional development, education, and expertise of horticultural therapy practitioners.

During the last decade, there has been increased interest in therapeutic gardens. These gardens are designed for health care, rehabilitative, and other therapeutic settings. The American Society of Landscape Architects maintains a professional practice network of consultants who specialize in designing therapeutic gardens. These purposefully designed gardens facilitate interaction with the healing elements of nature and promote four seasons of sensory stimulation and a wealth of therapeutic metaphors. Various types of gardens include healing gardens, rehabilitation gardens, and restorative gardens.

The calming environment of the garden can help relieve symptoms associated with depression, stress, and anxiety. Horticultural therapy has been shown to help improve memory, cognitive abilities, and language skills and promote socialization. A meta-analysis of the health effects of gardening and horticulture revealed a wide range of health benefits including increases in life satisfaction, quality of life, and self-esteem (Soga et al., 2016).

Some clinicians hold sessions in gardens that are available right outside their office door. If a client enjoys gardening at their home or at a community garden, the clinician might consider writing a nature prescription that encourages the client to spend time there and engage in interactions that are appropriate for the season and/or address a particular issue on which the client is working. Rich in metaphors and interaction patterns, the garden can be a deeply healing space.

Care Farms

Care farms offer therapeutic interventions, social support, skills development, and engagement with nature and agriculture. These programs occur on working farms and include engagement with the land, plants, animals, and other farm workers. Care farms serve a diverse population including individuals with intellectual and developmental disabilities, veterans, older people with dementia, people experiencing traumatic grief, and those in recovery from addiction. The calming effect of being outdoors in nature and the meaningful engagement of farming activity contribute to the therapeutic outcomes, lessen social isolation, and foster a sense of resilience and environmental steward-ship. Care farming has been popular in the U.K. and other parts of Europe for decades, but is just emerging as a therapeutic alternative in the United States.

Forest Bathing: Shinrin-Yoku

Forest bathing is a mindfulness practice that involves taking in the forest with all our senses. Forest bathing encourages us to be fully present by slowing our pace, unplugging from technology, and inten-tionally engaging our senses with the natural environment around us. Going for a walk in the woods to clear our mind isn't new. But taking the time to do so isn't as common as it once was. I recently read an article that asked how we got to the point where a walk in the woods needed to be branded as bathing and sold as a form of well-being. The answer, in part, lies in the sheer numbers of us that inhabit the planet and live in cities. According to the World Bank, the urban popula-tion worldwide grew from 751 million in 1950 to 4.4 billion in 2023. That means that 56% of the world's population lives in urban centers where access to nature—and a daily walk through it—can no longer be taken for granted. The term shinrin-yoku emerged in the 1980s in Japan, where 93% of the population lives in cities. The purpose then was to offer an antidote to tech-boon burnout, address stress among Japanese men, and encourage residents to reconnect with the country's forests to protect them. Forest bathing is now a pillar of preventative health care in Japan, where the government has poured millions of dollars into forest bathing research that seems to prove its beneficial effects.

During the COVID-19 pandemic, forest bathing became popu-lar in the United States as people searched for ways to calm their stress and connect outdoors while social distancing. But this prac-tice is proving to be more than a trendy activity. Research findings show that forest bathing has numerous health benefits. In one meta-analysis, researchers reviewed 971 articles and found that forest bathing effectively reduced serum and salivary cortisol levels, indicating its potential to reduce stress. Another meta-analysis reviewed studies where forest bathing was introduced to urban dwellers. Not only did the practice reduce their stress, but it also significantly lowered their blood pressure. Research has shown that 2 hours of time spent immersed in the forest environment can also improve memory and concentration and reduce anxiety, depression, anger, and fatigue. Studies have also shown that forest bathing improves immune function. As we walk in the forest beneath the trees, we inhale phytoncides, substances released by trees, which have antimicrobial properties that can boost our immune system and increase natural killer cell activity.

Forest bathing emphasizes taking in the forest environment with your senses in order to be fully present in the moment. Examples of prompts might be:

- Notice how sunlight filters through the leaves
- Feel the textures of the various tree trunks
- Listen for birdsong or wildlife
- Taste the freshness in the air by sucking in air as if you are sucking a straw
- Breathe in the fragrances of the forest

As clinicians move therapy outdoors and prescribe time in nature to their clients, forest bathing may offer ideas to enrich those experiences.

Wilderness Therapy and Adventure Therapy Programs

Wilderness therapy and adventure therapy programs are generally not thought of as a form of ecotherapy. As with any emerging field, there has been some confusion about what practices constitute the various treatment modalities. For the individual clinician, I think it is important to be familiar with the various nature-based treatment modalities and be able to refer a client to an appropriate alternative if necessary. I leave it to my colleagues to sort out what treatment offering is a subset of another. I mention wilderness therapy and adventure therapy here because they are offered in the outdoors and share some overlapping areas of theory with ecopsychology but have characteristics that make them distinct from the practice of ecotherapy.

Both wilderness therapy and adventure therapy are primarily offered to at-risk youth and adolescents as treatment options for behavioral disorders, substance abuse, and other mental health issues. Other populations are served by these programs as well including veterans recovering from trauma, childhood cancer survivors, and people with diabetes. Wilderness therapy and adventure therapy programs are conducted in a group format and generally in a remote setting. Creating community among the participants while being removed from their daily lives is a central component to these programs. Another characteristic that makes them distinct from the practice of ecotherapy is that they have an overnight stay element and generally take place over an extended period of time ranging from several days to several months and beyond. The programs utilize various outdoor activities to promote personal and interpersonal growth and development.

SPECIAL POPULATIONS

As we have seen, ecotherapy can be incorporated into a variety of settings, is compatible with many traditional theories and practices, and enhances therapeutic work with individuals. In this section, I highlight several special populations for which ecotherapy can be especially effective in treatment.

Veterans

For veterans returning from military service, experiencing nature through outdoor recreation can play an important role in reducing stress and trauma-related symptoms. Several group programs such as Huts for Vets, Outward Bound, and Warrior Expeditions offer adventure therapy and adaptive sports. Ecotherapy can be a good addition to a treatment plan for the veteran looking to address issues of PTSD in a more traditional setting. Some local VA programs offer day hikes, canoe trips, and fly-fishing experiences that are facilitated by mental health professionals trained in ecotherapy methods. Quality time in a positive environment with supportive people is essential for recovery, and the solitude of nature offers a healing setting. The individual clinician working with a veteran may consider moving sessions outdoors after assessing their appropriateness for outdoor work and thoroughly discussing the risks and benefits.

Ecotherapy for Specific Health Concerns

Ecotherapeutic methods can be incorporated into treatment planning for patients with health-related concerns. I include a few examples here, and I invite the reader to consider other health issues from their practice that might benefit.

Patients in Memory Care. Patients in memory care facilities and their families often struggle with finding activities that bring connection and joy. Several years ago, I volunteered to consult at a memory care facility as they were completing their outdoor space where residents could safely take a walk or sit in the sunshine. The area was enclosed, level, and had wide walking paths that were paved so that a person assisted by a walker or wheelchair could safely navigate. The paths were circular and led back to the door of the building, so there was no fear of getting lost. Raised beds for planting flowers and quick growing vegetables were added. To see the spark of recognition and a smile from a patient as she held a tomato warmed from the sun, and hear her recollection of growing tomatoes in her home garden was a delight. I saw adult family members moved to tears to see the joy on their loved one's face as they touched the colorful flowers, picked a ripe pepper, or planted a young basil plant.

Breast Cancer Survivors. Studies have shown that 42% of breast cancer survivors experience psychological distress and mood disorders during recovery, especially anxiety about cancer recurrence. It is often suggested to patients that they talk with other survivors. But some patients don't have friends or family members who have had breast cancer and may not have access to a support group or are unwilling to join one. Casting for Recovery is a national nonprofit organization that takes breast cancer survivors on weekend-long fly-fishing retreats. The goals extend well beyond teaching the participants to fly-fish, though. They hold group therapy sessions and pamper the guests with healthy meals and comfortable lodging, free of charge. Casting for Recovery was founded on the principles that the natural world is a healing force and that women who have survived breast cancer deserve one weekend free from the stresses of medical treatment, home, and work to experience something new and challenging in a safe and beautiful environment. The volunteers who help staff the retreats include medical providers and psychosocial professionals, fly-fishing instructors, and alumnae. The gentle motion of casting serves as physical therapy to those who have undergone surgery or radiation, while the sharing among participants provides emotional support and a renewed sense of purpose and priorities. For nearly 30 years, Casting for Recovery has provided healing fly-fishing retreats to more than 12,000 women across the country. In parts of the United States where fly-fishing is popular, there are local groups that offer lessons to women in recovery from breast cancer. Clinicians who treat breast cancer survivors might investigate whether a program is available in their local community. Clinicians with nature-based therapeutic skills can get involved by volunteering with such programs and by informing clients about them.

Prescribing Time in Nature for Heart Health. As we saw in Chapter 7, it is becoming more common for health care providers in the United States, Canada, and Europe to prescribe time in nature to their patients for preventative care and as treatment for some conditions. In a recent article published by the Preventive Cardiovascular Nurses Association, the health benefits from green space exposure are significant enough for practitioners and policy makers to recommend spending more time in nature to cardiac patients and those at risk for cardiovascular disease. Green space interventions like horticulture therapy, backyard gardening, and forest bathing are among the range of activities individuals are being prescribed for heart health.

It is well established that cardiovascular disease results from an interplay between genetic predisposition and environmental influences.

Environment and lifestyle are considered the primary influence. A recent study found cardiovascular disease risk was associated with residential greenness, specifically lower levels of sympathetic activation, reduced oxidative stress (i.e., the imbalance of free radicals and antioxidants that lead to cell damage) and higher angiogenic capacity (i.e., the ability to form new blood vessels, which aids in wound healing). These findings were independent of age, sex, race, smoking status, and neighborhood deprivation (Yeager et al., 2018). Green space exposure has been associated with other cardiovascular benefits including a decrease in heart rate, systolic and diastolic blood pressure, low-frequency heart rate variability, and stroke incidence and improved HDL cholesterol levels. The cardiovascular benefits from interacting with green space may be related to increased time spent outdoors in areas conducive to physical activity, which likely decreases stress levels. Lowering stress improves the prognosis in those with cardiovascular disease (Moxley, 2022).

Another opportunity for cardiac patients to gain exposure to green space is through participation in a Walk with a Doc program in their local community. This nonprofit organization was founded by a cardiologist, David Sabgir in 2005. Sabgir invited his patients to go for a walk with him in a local park on a Saturday morning in hopes of encouraging some behavior changes that were not happening by just talking about them in the clinical office. To his surprise, many patients and their families showed up, energized and ready to move. Today there are 500 chapters worldwide including Walk with a Future Doc chapters led by medical students and Just Walk chapters led by other licensed health care providers. During the walking session, the provider gives a brief presentation on a health topic and then leads participants on a walk at their own pace while being available for informal discussion and questions. These sessions also model the behavior the provider is intending to encourage—moving our bodies in nature. Clinicians can check with their local hospital or clinic to see if such a program is offered in their area. Writing a prescription for a client to get out and take a Walk with a Doc might be the encouragement they need to participate.

Clinicians can also prescribe other ways to spend time in nature for their clients who are at risk for cardiovascular disease or who are recovering from a cardiovascular event. Encouraging the client to interact with the affordances of nature nearby, such as taking a walk in the woods or local park, planting a small garden or tending potted plants on a deck, and leaving technology behind and mindfully experiencing nature around them may aid in their recovery or help to lower their risk.

Climate Change Scientists, Educators, and Advocates

Climate change represents one of the greatest challenges of our time. It is not just an environmental problem, it is also a psychological problem. The mental health impacts of climate change are just beginning to be researched and addressed in clinics, schools, and therapy offices. The next chapter focuses on the role of therapy in the face of climate change. Here I want to highlight those working on the front lines: the climate scientists who bear witness to the destruction of ecosystems firsthand and have to manage the implications of what the science is showing them, the environmental science educators and students who are immersed in this information as they prepare for their future, and the climate advocates who sound the alarm and deliver the message for change who too often are rebuffed or not believed. These folks represent a special population for which ecotherapy may have something unique to offer.

The growing body of research around the intersection of climate change and mental health rarely addresses the climate scientists' experience. When it does, the results are concerning. Only 6% of the 380 lead authors and editors for the Intergovernmental Panel on Climate Change (IPCC) think that the 1.5° warming limit set by the 2015 Paris Agreement is achievable, and most said they felt distress and frustration over how the climate crisis is being addressed worldwide (Rodrigues, 2024). Climate scientists are grappling with the realities of what the science is telling them about our rapidly changing world, the expectation of coming up with solutions, and the painfully slow process of cultural change to address it. The emotions often expressed include deep sadness, frustration, grief, loss, anxiety, fear, depression, and feelings of helplessness and hopelessness. The stress that climate scientists experience is similar to what first responders experience in climate disasters. Both groups are exposed to the realities of climate change in very profound ways.

As I put the finishing touches on the final draft of this book, a new administration has taken over the federal government in the United States. Among the first actions taken were executive orders withdrawing the U.S. from the Paris Climate Agreement and the World Health Organization, and reversing many policies at the federal level related to climate change. Support for research on climate and health, climate adaptation, and preparedness for climate disasters will likely decline significantly. These actions by the federal government will place an added burden on those grappling with these challenging issues.

The Climate Psychiatry Alliance, an independent group of psychiatrists and mental health professionals based in San Francisco, California, has joined forces with a similar group, the Climate Psychology Alliance North America, to develop a climate-awareness training program for therapists. One approach that can especially benefit climate scientists is group discussions that enable them to feel safe to share their thoughts and feelings and help them realize they are not alone, according to Robin Cooper, a member of the steering committee at the Climate Psychiatry Alliance (Rodrigues, 2024). Other approaches involve building psychological resilience, holding space for hope, and mindfulness training. Clinicians who are climate-aware and possess a skill set in nature-based methods are in a unique position to help those on the front line of the climate crisis.

CONCLUSION

This chapter covered the unique ethical concerns that come when we step out of the traditional office setting and offer nature-based methods to our clients in local parks, in gardens and care farms, on walking trails, and in forests. We reviewed a few forms of ecotherapy including animal-assisted therapy and green space interventions and made a distinction between ecotherapy and adventure and wilderness therapies. We also looked at a few special populations for whom ecotherapy can be utilized to help address trauma, health-related concerns, and the distress of a changing world. We introduced several organizations that clinicians might get involved with or consider as a resource for their clients. The next chapter looks at ecotherapy's role in addressing the climate situation we face.

10

THERAPY IN THE FACE OF CLIMATE CHANGE

I opened this book with my personal story of surviving the Holiday Farm Fire, a devastating wildfire that swept through the McKenzie Valley in Oregon in 2020, burning 173,393 acres. It was one of the largest wildfires in Oregon history. But that event was only one of 30 simultaneous wildfires that impacted the state that fall in what became known as the 2020 Labor Day Wildfires. The multiple wildfires burned 1.2 million acres of land (twice the annual average), forced more than 40,000 people to evacuate their homes, destroyed 5,000 homes and businesses, and claimed nine lives, producing the most devastating sequence of simultaneous wildfires in state history. Fueled by prolonged dry conditions (not what the Pacific Northwest is known for historically), drought, a critically dry ecosystem, and a historic wind event, the fires created record amounts of burned trees, ash, and debris that contributed to landslides, rockfalls, and substantial structural destruction to several state highways. The 2020 Labor Day Wildfires have proven to be the most expensive disaster in Oregon's history (Oregon Department of Transportation, 2022).

Working in devastated physical environments for long hours, combined with the stress associated with the COVID-19 pandemic and the emotional strain of interacting directly with wildfire-impacted homeowners and communities, the cleanup and recovery effort took its toll on the people doing the restoration work over the following months. According to the post-disaster summary report by the state's

Department of Transportation, nearly all field and leadership staff reported some type of mental health challenge during the sustained 14-month emergency response operation. Although there were support services available during the recovery operations including staff and peer support, as well as emotional support dogs, most staff did not have the time to take advantage of these services (Oregon Department of Transportation, 2022). These hidden costs to residents, first responders, and after-disaster clean-up and recovery personnel are rarely reported or considered when we think about the costs of climate-related disasters.

As I write this chapter in September 2024, my phone dings with an app update on the wildfire that has been burning only 7 miles away from Blue River, the community destroyed by the Holiday Farm Fire in 2020. The current fire is consolidated with six other active fires and together they have burned 6,676 acres so far. With each ding of the app, I react and check my phone.

Being attuned to the weather conditions, sleeping with the phone on the nightstand each night in case there is an evacuation, and keeping the Go Bags within reach in the garage, has become a way of life during fire season for many people living in the western United States and in other places around the world. Others experience such concerns related to hurricanes, tornadoes, flooding, and storm surges. As climate change impacts the outer landscape, people are experiencing a type of stress and a set of negative emotions that Australian environmentalist and professor Glenn Albrecht (2012) called "solastalgia." This concept names the environmentally induced distress that is produced by environmental change impacting people in their home place. Solastalgia is a feeling of melancholia about the chronic deterioration of a loved home environment. It is a form of homesickness—a longing for home, as what was once familiar becomes unpredictable. Albrecht delineated a range of "psychoterratic" syndromes—mental health impacts associated with environmental damage and change (p. 250). We will explore more of these later in this chapter.

Climate change represents one of the greatest challenges of our time. The consequences of climate change have serious effects on both human health and planetary health. While 2023 was recorded as the hottest year on record globally (NOAA,2024), 2024 is lining up to replace that record. Climate change is a serious threat. Several researchers have described climate change as an *existential threat*, reflecting how deeply it impacts our core understandings and the current social system, if not life itself. The threat to our core understandings can be described as a potential loss of ontological security—a feeling that one's knowledge and the systems of understanding that one has relied on are no longer true (Clayton, 2020).

PSYCHOLOGY'S ROLE IN ADDRESSING OUR CHANGING CLIMATE

The discipline of psychology has been involved in addressing environmental issues for decades. Since the middle of the 20th century, environmental psychologists have worked to understand what motivates environmentally sustainable behavior. Just a few years ago, most psychology articles about climate change focused on changing behaviors to mitigate human effects on the environment, most specifically aimed at reducing our carbon footprint through the reduction of fossil fuel use. To address widespread climate denial, psychology has been involved in developing the messaging about the warming planet.

More recently, clinicians and other mental health providers are exploring ways to encourage adaptation to our changing world. These include motivating actions to create defensible space around homes to prevent wildfire losses, to make buildings more resistant to flooding, and to adjust agricultural practices to account for new climate conditions.

Most recently, the psychological literature is focused on how to cope with the acute trauma caused by climate-related disasters that have increased in frequency and severity and on the psychological impacts of chronic stress related to climate change. Empirical evidence indicates that both acute and chronic mental health effects of climate change, including posttraumatic stress disorder, depression, anxiety, suicidal ideations, and grief, have risen sharply in the last decade (Cunsolo et al., 2020).

Psychology has also contributed to the conversation about the connection of climate change and climate justice—specifically, how climate change impacts vulnerable populations who live in fragile and often degraded parts of the world, those who have fewer resources to protect themselves from the impacts of climate change, and those who rely most closely on the land for their livelihood and well-being such as Indigenous Peoples and farmers.

At this point, the field of psychology is deeply involved in addressing climate change through working with interdisciplinary task forces and governmental groups to promote environmental sustainability, to address behavioral adaptations, and to highlight the mental health impacts of climate change. Psychologists are now involved with the Intergovernmental Panel on Climate Change (IPCC) and a growing number of mental health providers are joining with others to collaborate on addressing climate-related problems and solutions.

This chapter focuses on addressing the issue of climate change on a more intimate level. Specifically, how does the individual clinician address the chronic psychological impacts of climate change? Do we recognize the chronic stressors and emotions that are in response to the gradual effects of climate change that are often not articulated by clients? *Are we asking the right questions?* In this chapter, I present recent research on people's perspectives on climate change. I discuss how the practices and methods of ecotherapy might be useful in the clinician's work as we approach this pervasive topic with our clients and patients in a meaningful way. This chapter also looks at what promotes climate resilience and encourages preparedness. It concludes with a discussion of the clinician's role in advocating for the mental health impacts of climate change.

To begin, I'd like to ask the reader: How do *you* respond to climate change? How do you think about it? What do you feel about it? How have you personally been touched by it? What have you seen in your clients, patients, students, family members, colleagues, or fellow activists? Climate change is global, pervasive, and ongoing. Clinicians are asked to address the emotional impacts of climate change even as they, too, are impacted. We are all in this together.

By The Numbers: Perspectives on Climate Change

As the effects of climate change become more evident, 56% of U.S. adults say climate change is the most important issue facing us today, according to a 2020 survey of 2,017 adults conducted by The Harris Poll on behalf of the American Psychological Association. At the time of the survey, more than two-thirds (68%) of adults said that they had at least a little ecoanxiety, defined as any anxiety or worry about climate change and its effects (APA, 2020).

In another 2020 survey of 1000 adults by ecoAmerica and Lake Research Partners, 74% of Americans report being concerned about climate change (including 45% who were very concerned), but only 59% believe others around them are concerned about it. The report concluded that the gap in actual versus perceived climate concern could be contributing to silence on the issue (Buttel et al., 2020). That gap might also be contributing to the isolation many feel about their concerns, leading to some of the mental health issues highlighted in this chapter.

Ecoanxiety, sometimes called climate anxiety, is defined by the APA as "a chronic fear of environmental doom" (Schreiber, 2021). It can show up in a range of emotions, most commonly as fear, anxiety, worry, stress, grief, or a sense of hopelessness about the future. There is growing evidence suggesting the number of people distressed about the impacts of climate change is increasing rapidly. In a representative survey conducted in the United States in December 2022, of the 70% of participants that said they were at least "somewhat worried" about climate change, 26% reported they were "alarmed"—these rates doubling from the previous 10 years. A poll conducted in the U.K. reported that 85% of the respondents were "concerned" about climate change, and of these 52% were "very concerned" (Pitt et al., 2024).

Some evidence suggests that climate anxiety is more prevalent among young people. A 2021 study gathered quantitative global data on a large scale. Researchers surveyed 10,000 young people aged 16–25 in 10 countries (Australia, Brazil, Finland, France, India, Nigeria, Philippines, Portugal, the U.K., and the United States, with 1000 participants per country). Respondents across all countries were worried about climate change with 59% very or extremely worried, and 84% were at least moderately worried. More than 50% reported each of the following emotions: sad, anxious, angry, powerless, helpless, and guilty. More than 45% of the respondents said their feelings about climate change negatively affected their daily life and functioning; 75% said they think the future is frightening, and 83% said that they think people have failed to take care of the planet. Respondents also rated governmental responses to climate change negatively and reported associated feelings of betrayal (Hickman et al., 2021). This study showed that the psychological burdens of climate change are being felt by large proportions of young people around the world. Distress about climate change is associated with young people perceiving that they have no future, that humanity is doomed, and that the governments are failing to respond, leaving feelings of betrayal and abandonment by adults. These are chronic stressors that could have long-lasting impacts on the mental health of young people.

The emotions associated with climate change are a fast-growing topic of research. It is incumbent on clinicians to be aware of the current literature on the psychological impacts of this pervasive influence in our lives. This chapter reminds us that the foundational principles and theories of ecopsychology and the practices and methods of ecotherapy are essential to address the psychological impacts of climate change with our clients and patients. Additionally, climate-aware clinicians have much to offer in collaborations with other health care providers, community leaders, educators, local governments, and climate advocates to prepare and strengthen social networks and infuse mental health impacts into action plans and policies.

Psychological Responses to Climate Change

The psychological impacts of climate change can be categorized into two broad types: the acute trauma of living through a climate-related disaster like a hurricane, flooding, wildfire, or drought and the chronic anxiety that comes with knowing that the ecosystem that we depend upon for survival is in trouble. The psychological impacts of discrete events like natural disasters have been studied for decades, and studies show increased levels of PTSD, depression, anxiety, substance abuse, and domestic violence among survivors of natural disasters. These effects are lessened by sources of social support and personal resilience, and amplified by the devastating losses of homes, loved ones, and livelihood. There are specific emotions connected to living through these natural disasters and their aftermath. Not believing that "it could happen here" is a common first response. Fear of another climate-related event is pervasive among survivors and is one form of ecoanxiety.

But even among people who have not experienced such disasters, simple awareness of the problem may be accompanied by emotions that include fear, anger, feelings of powerlessness, and emotional exhaustion. These negative emotions do not constitute mental illness, but watching the seemingly irrevocable impacts of climate change unfold can leave us worried about the future for ourselves, our children, and future generations, and may lead to feelings of stress, sadness, grief, and even guilt. The feeling of uncertainty about the future is arguably one of the central aspects of climate change (Clayton, 2020).

There are many ways to think about the emotional responses to the changing landscape. Central to this idea is the ecopsychological tenet that our inner world and the outer world are intimately connected. In Chapter 2, I introduced Roszak's (1992) concept of the ecological unconscious as one of the foundational tenets of ecopsychology that relates to ecotherapy. You will recall that Roszak identified the ecological unconscious as the deepest substratum of Jung's collective unconscious. Roszak conceptualized the ecological unconscious as the repository of an evolutionary record that ties the human psyche to the universe's full cosmic history. This concept reminds us that unconscious processes exist within us, and as practitioners we are trained in understanding these intrapsychic processes as they relate to other people, especially our early caregivers and our partners. The ecological unconscious extends our intrapsychic processes to the earth itself—specifically, the processes of identification and repression. Traditional therapy seeks to heal the alienation between individuals, while ecotherapy seeks to heal the alienation between the person and the natural world. According to Roszak, repression of the ecological unconscious is the deepest root of our environmental crisis, and open access to the ecological unconscious is the path to sanity (Roszak, 1992). Through identification within the ecological unconscious, humans recognize their ethical responsibility to the planet as clearly as we experience our ethical responsibility to other people. Human health and planetary health are interdependent. At some deep level, *we just know* the planet is suffering. As clinicians, we must find ways to address this deep knowing and bring it to consciousness so that we can use our full creative energies to address the environmental crisis.

Australian philosopher and environmentalist Glenn Albrecht (2012) identified a range of psychoterratic syndromes that he defined as a constellation of mental health impacts associated with environmental degradation. Psychoterratic syndromes include not only solastalgia (the feelings associated with the chronic deterioration of a loved home environment), but also ecoanxiety (a nonspecific worry about the negative trends concerning the environment and the climate) and ecoparalysis (the inability to respond to the ecological challenges due to a perception that they are intractable). Albrecht argues that we need a relevant psychoterratic language to understand and respond meaningfully to the ecocultural challenges of the 21st century. Albrecht notes that compared to Indigenous cultures, the language of English-speaking cultures has few concepts that describe the psychodynamics of the human–nature relationship. He suggests that we need to be able to put into words a description of both positive and negative relationships to place and landscape in order to overcome the inertia, anxiety, and paralysis that are prevalent in contemporary society, especially as we confront the pervasive changes brought about by climate change.

As clinicians, how do we approach these powerful emotions in our work? Do our clients and patients see the therapeutic session as a place to bring up their thoughts and feelings related to climate change? If we expand our lens to include the relationship the client has with the natural world, as we discussed in Chapter 3, do we ask about their concerns for the planet? Do we consider a client's connection to their homeplace? Recognizing the disruption to a person's environmental identity or to their attachment to place, and naming it, can be a great relief to the client.

EcoAmerica's 2024 American Climate Perspectives Survey

indicated that Americans are ready and eager for health professionals to advance climate action. The majority of participants (69%) expressed strong trust in health professionals for information on climate change and guidance on how to protect their health from the physical and mental health impacts of climate change (Speiser & Ishaq, 2024).

Many mental health providers are trained to treat patients with trauma, substance abuse, relationship issues, family discord, and any number of other challenging topics. But most clinicians are not trained on how to address the psychological impacts of our current environmental situation. This lack of preparation can lead some practitioners to avoid asking the questions posed above. Others look for research related to the intersection of climate change and psychology, which is scattered across multiple journals and in a variety of fields of study. Even those of us who for decades have focused our work on connecting patients with nature and understand the research on how that can be good for mental health are left with the void of evidenced-based practices on how to address the psychological impacts of climate change. Fortunately, during the last several years, a number of professional groups have emerged that offer the opportunity to share information including Climate Rx, the Alliance of Climate Therapists–Northwest, the collaboration of the American Psychological Association and ecoAmerica, Planetary Health Alliance, Climate Psychology Alliance, Climate Psychiatry Alliance, and others.

The next section looks at themes that are emerging in the literature that help to shape best practices for treatment of climate-related emotions and mental health interventions.

The Research on Therapeutic Interventions for Climate-Related Emotions

Research into therapeutic interventions to address climate-related emotions such as ecoanxiety is at a fairly early stage. One of the emerging tenets of climate psychology is that clinicians should validate the client's climate-related emotions as reasonable, not pathological or irrational. Defining feelings like fear, anxiety, grief, and shame as rational responses to a world in peril can allow clients to feel heard, understood, and not so isolated. When we are treating a client with anxiety, one goal of treatment is to understand how much of their anxiety is internally generated and perhaps out of proportion to the reality of a situation. Ecoanxiety poses a different challenge because the client's worries may be rational and evidence-based, but they feel isolated or frustrated because those around them may dismiss them as overreacting or voice their disapproval due to the current social polarization on the topic of climate change. The resulting self-silencing may heighten their anxiety and inhibit social connections that can be powerful sources of resilience.

Uncertainty, unpredictability, and uncontrollability are three fundamental characteristics of climate change that contribute to ecoanxiety. The condition can overlap with generalized anxiety disorder and other mental health disorders in response to a felt threat. Experiences of ecoanxiety often include dystopian thoughts about the future; negative and sometimes intense emotions of fear, anger, dread, guilt, grief, and despair; and behavioral manifestations such as sleep disturbances and panic attacks. Ecoanxiety is currently not considered a mental health disorder and has no formal guidelines for clinical diagnosis or treatment. The condition does represent a set of responses ranging from normal reactions to a serious environmental threat to more overwhelmed states that can impair daily functioning. Severe ecoanxiety can overlap with clinical mental health disorders that may require evaluation and treatment (Wang et al., 2023).

Current research identifies three coping strategies in climate anxiety intervention: problem-solving coping, emotion-focused coping, and meaning-focused coping. Problem-solving coping involves pro-environmental behaviors to mitigate personal effects on the climate such as reducing fossil fuel use, composting, recycling, and joining with others in work on societal causes of climate change. This coping strategy has the benefit of fostering actions by the individual that may lead to feelings of empowerment. Emotion-focused coping involves strategies to manage uncomfortable feelings related to climate anxiety such as talking with others, expressing emotions, reframing to de-emphasize the threat, and distractions. This strategy may reduce the anxiety in the short term, but it is unlikely to be effective over the long term since there are no actions involved to mitigate the root causes of climate change. Meaning-focused coping involves strategies to reappraise the situation by focusing on progress being made over time to address climate change, the number of people working toward constructive change, and the abundance of knowledge that now exists on the topic (Pitt et al., 2023). In other words, put the problem into historical perspective in an attempt to find hope by trusting that society will find solutions through science, technology, and so on. Research suggests participants who use meaning-focused coping reported higher life satisfaction, well-being, reduced anxiety, positive feelings, and higher levels of climate engagement and self-efficacy compared to those who tend to rely only on emotion- and problem-focused strategies (Pitt et al., 2023). Both meaning-focused and emotion-focused strategies can involve hope. The meaning-focused coping strategies may serve to facilitate individual well-being while allowing for engagement in behaviors to address the problem (Clayton, 2020). These findings are important considerations in the development of climate anxiety interventions. These studies also suggest that incorporating a combination of coping strategies into climate anxiety interventions may be most effective.

A 2023 study of 230 participants who identified as "professionals with an interest in climate anxiety" presented the participants with a range of interventions for climate anxiety that have been discussed in the literature. For each intervention, they were asked to endorse whether they believed the intervention could support, trigger, or prolong climate anxiety for an individual. Participants could choose as many options as they agreed with. The interventions that received the highest endorsements as interventions to address climate anxiety included:

Nature connection: 90%
Mindfulness and/or meditation practice: 84%
Engaging in climate justice activism: 86%
Engagement in pro-environmental behaviors: 83%

Interestingly, 89% thought engaging with news or social media would be triggering for climate anxiety and 75% thought it would prolong it (Pitt et al., 2024).

In recent scoping reviews (i.e., overviews of literature), connecting individuals to nature is a prevalent theme for exploring climate anxiety interventions. The encouraging results from this research suggest a significant potential for the nature-based approaches of ecotherapy to address the intersection of climate change and mental health.

Practical Considerations for the Clinician

From a pragmatic point of view, how might clinicians address the chronic stressors, profound losses, and powerful emotions associated with climate change? For many clinicians, the issues of climate change are rarely the presenting problem when a client comes to the office. Yet rates of depression are on the rise, along with an increase in anxiety and suicide. Perhaps it is time to ask if there is a possible connection (Hasbach, 2015). Depending on where you practice, you might be seeing more cases of concern for the environment come through your office door. How might therapy be instrumental in providing a forum for people to address the deep and often unacknowledged feelings associated with the environmental situation, so that energy can be redirected to creative, solution-oriented endeavors?

It is important to remember that many methods in the clinician's toolbox may be useful in addressing emotions associated with climate change, as well as many of the ecotherapy methods discussed in earlier chapters. The clinician can include questions about environmental concerns as part of the intake questions. We can ask about whether the client has been directly impacted by climate-related weather events. If so, we can ask about their coping strategies. Clinicians can draw on our knowledge of stress reduction theory and attention restoration theory as we work with clients to lessen the impacts of stress associated with climate change. Ecotherapists are comfortable with moving therapy sessions outdoors and with prescribing time outdoors to their clients. Cocreating outdoor experiences for direct interactions with nature can be therapeutic, especially with an eye to noticing the resiliency of nature. Incorporating therapeutic nature language into discussions and into nature prescriptions fosters intentional nature engagement, which has been shown to create meaning, facilitate coping, and decrease stress. Cocreating rituals with a client or a community to address ecological grief at the loss of a beloved place is another method the ecotherapist might offer. Becoming a climate-aware clinician and adding the methods and practices of ecotherapy puts the clinician in a solid position to help their clients and patients acknowledge their feelings related to climate change, create a coping plan, develop resilience, and foster a sense of agency.

By becoming climate-aware, the clinician can sharpen their focus on how issues of climate concern might impact their work with couples. If the individuals in a committed relationship hold different values around lifestyle choices that have environmental impacts, they may identify those lifestyle choices as sources of stress in the relationship. In my practice I have had several couples address their differing views about the environmental costs of travel, consumerism, energy use, and recycling/reusing items. Environmental concerns have been raised by couples as they discuss where to live. Other couples have discussed whether to bring a child into a world where there is an uncertain future. Still others have worked through the decision of whether to expand their existing family.

Clinicians who are climate-aware can also offer parents guidance in how to talk to their kids about climate change. It is important that children get *age-appropriate* information about such big issues. When kids are exposed to these complex issues and have no agency to do anything about it, they are left feeling frightened, overwhelmed, or depressed. Worse yet, they may develop apathy as a way of coping. When parents express concern about a child's anxiety, I ask them about their family's connection (or disconnection) to nature. Young people need to have the opportunity to learn about their home ground and feel a connection to nature that they can regularly access. Nature immersion helps kids love nature before they must do the hard work of trying to save it. Kids need the opportunity to experience a kinship with nature, to develop their environmental identity, and to feel grounded in a particular place. They need to develop a deep, sincere connection to the part of themselves that recognizes that they, too, are a part of the natural world.

I also inquire about how much time their child spends with digital technology. Research demonstrates that most kids spend far more time connected with screens than with the natural world. On average, today's kids spend up to 44 hours per week in front of a screen, and fewer than 10 minutes a day playing outdoors. We know that a high level of digital connection can exacerbate anxiety and stress in us all. Clinicians attuned to the challenges of engaging kids with nature find ample resources to share with parents through books, local outdoor programs for families, and international organizations like the Children and Nature Network (www.childrenandnaturenetwork.org).

Building Resilience and Encouraging Preparedness

Clinicians will find various levels of awareness, concern, and preparedness for climate change depending on where you live and practice. Individuals, families, health care providers, policy makers, community leaders, and human service organizations can all help to build individual and community-wide resilience with shared responsibility to address solutions to climate change in order to protect mental health and well-being. Visible leadership, making the health and climate connection, and involvement by health professionals can increase support for solutions and lessen issues of partisanship (Clayton, Manning et al., 2021).

Solutions start with building individual resilience, something that mental health providers can facilitate. Clinicians can assist clients in fostering hope, identifying and cultivating coping skills, bolstering interpersonal sources of support, and finding meaning in life—all factors in building one's resilience capacity. Therapeutic work can encourage action on personal preparedness for themselves and their families and on maintaining a connection to place and community. By expanding the scope of treatment to include the human–nature relationship, ecotherapists and climate-aware mental health professionals can fully address the complexity of their clients' issues, support clients' behavior changes toward nature, help them build resilience, and help them discover ways to cope with the emotional impacts of climate change.

Societal changes needed to address climate change require multilevel governance, policies, institutional will, and financial investment—all with an eye to social justice and mental health considerations. We all have a role to play. The key is to recognize one's sphere of influence and be willing to add our voice, engage our creative energy, and risk speaking our truth.

Health care professionals and mental health practitioners have a unique and powerful role in influencing patients, professional communities, the public discourse, and policy makers on the intersection of human health and planetary health. The next chapter looks at what ecopsychology and ecotherapy might contribute in that regard. We'll also explore future directions for the practice of ecotherapy.

11

FUTURE DIRECTIONS
FOR ECOTHERAPY

We have seen how the practices and methods of ecotherapy are more relevant today than ever before. With the growing awareness of the impacts of climate-related anxiety and trauma and mounting evidence that direct contact with nature has powerful psychological and emotional benefits, addressing the relationship between humans and the natural world should be considered a best practice. This final chapter examines future directions for the field of ecopsychology and the practice of ecotherapy. We will also look at the unique role ecotherapists have in addressing the intersection of human health and planetary health.

EXPANDING THE REACH OF ECOTHERAPY

When practitioners expand their scope of treatment beyond human-to-human relationships, to recognize and acknowledge the human–nature relationship, the therapeutic process is broadened and deepened, and the client is seen holistically. Research results support the assertion that interacting with nature is *vital* to our physical and psychological health and well-being. In Chapter 2, I highlighted studies showing that interactions with nature produced a broad range of positive psychological benefits including reductions in stress, anxiety, and depression, as well as increased relaxation, focused attention, self-esteem, mood, and confidence. These benefits were seen across the lifespan. Regular interactions with nature are consistently associated with mental health benefits for children and adolescents including improvements in emotional well-being and reduced depression and ADHD symptoms. Likewise, studies of older adults showed reduced depression and anxiety and improved cognitive function. It can be argued that spending time in nature has a salutogenic effect, acting as a buffer between the stresses of daily life and our mental health (Gray et al., 2024).

Being outdoors in nature also shapes behaviors that encourage adults and children to be physically active and to have social interactions with others, which can have important benefits for those with anxiety and depression. These outdoor behaviors can also combat loneliness, promote a sense of collective identity and a sense of place, and contribute to individual and community resilience. Some countries have prioritized the reconnection of people to the natural environment as a key public health strategy. Ecological perspectives have informed the development of health-promotion initiatives and practices such as healthy cities, schools, and workplaces.

Research evidence shines a light on the need to incorporate the natural world into our therapeutic work by assessing a client's access to green and blue spaces, by inquiring about their historical and current connection with nature, by understanding their environmental identity and their sense of place, and by asking about their experiences and concerns related to climate change. Moving the therapy session outdoors and/or encouraging nature interactions by writing nature prescriptions sends powerful messages of support for the importance of the human–nature connection.

Mental health clinicians who utilize nature-based methods should consider developing collaborative alliances with health care providers practicing nature-based medicine. Recall from Chapter 7 that nature-based medicine is defined as the prescriptive, evidence-based use of natural settings and nature-based interventions, with the mission to prevent and treat disease and improve well-being (La Puma, 2023). Studies have shown that nature-based interventions used as preventive tools in medicine have produced these results:

- An intentional walk in a park may be as effective as Ritalin for childhood ADHD
- Those with greater nature exposure had fewer episodes of depression and anxiety during the COVID-19 pandemic
- Walking in a forest exposed to evergreens' phytoncides enhances natural killer cell activity and lowers blood pressure and interleukin-6 activity
- Gardening daily may reduce risk factors for dementia by 36%. Patients with dementia who have access to stimulatory gardens are less likely to fall or suffer loss of an activity of daily living than those without access
- Greater soil biodiversity appears to act as a barrier to antibiotic resistance
- Nature-related activities improve the gut microbiota and fecal serotonin of preschool children (LaPuma, 2023)

It is clear that nature contact offers promise both for prevention and treatment of many health challenges that are public health priorities including cardiovascular disease, cancer, depression, anxiety, and obesity. Evidence also suggests that nature contact is associated with well-being and happiness.

Although research has identified many associations between nature contact and health, much remains to be learned. Collaborations between clinicians and researchers can help to identify and investigate the underlying pathways and causal mechanisms involved between nature and human well-being. Such collaborative research should focus on characterizing associations in ways that are relevant to clinical practice. For example, how is nature contact associated with specific health outcomes of public health importance? How do these associations vary across different populations, life stages, and so on (Frumkin et al., 2017)?

La Puma (2023) identified some of the challenges of the emerging nature-based medical field including whether health care providers will be able to get the additional education and training in nature-based medicine, access evidence-based research, practice the skills needed to meet patient needs, and be compensated for their work. These challenges parallel those faced by mental health clinicians practicing ecotherapy.

Nature-informed mental health clinicians are working with pediatricians and family physicians to have nature interventions recognized and compensated by health insurance companies. Many of our counterparts in the U.K. and other countries around the world are far ahead of the United States in obtaining reimbursement for treatment modalities that include nature. In the United States, a clinical diagnosis is generally needed for insurance reimbursement. The current *Diagnostic and Statistical Manual* (*DSM-5-TR*) does not include the relationship between humans and the rest of nature. As we continue to see increased disconnection between people and nature and better understand the consequences of that disconnection, see symptoms of chronic anxiety in our patients related to climate change, and see acute trauma related to climate-related events, it is perhaps time to advocate for inclusion of these conditions in future versions of the *Diagnostic and Statistical Manual*. To be clear, the purpose of inclusion for these conditions is not to pathologize the acute and chronic psychological impacts of climate change, but to name them so that clinicians can provide supportive therapeutic services to their clients.

There is also a need for new training models for graduate students and mental health practitioners that include the human–nature relationship. Just as earlier training models were expanded to include our growing understanding of family systems and later our understanding of the impacts of societal norms and biases, we need to expand the scope of training to include the mental health impacts of connection or disconnection with the ecological system of which we are a part. Training models should map the evidence for nature-based interventions and include the acute and chronic impacts of climate change on mental health, since this pervasive factor is now an ongoing part of life. Training models should also include resilience training for providers and researchers.

Clinicians need to advocate for continued funding for research on the benefits of nature to mental health, especially for children. Research addressing cultural variations for nature-based interventions also needs further exploration. Interdisciplinary collaborations on research that demonstrates ecotherapy's efficacy as a therapeutic modality are vital, so that ecotherapy stands alongside other therapeutic modalities in the clinician's toolbox.

Rewilding Therapy

Addressing access to nature, discussing ways to systematically talk about nature interaction patterns (as in therapeutic nature language), and looking at ways to encourage direct nature experiences through outdoor sessions and nature prescriptions are important. Here, I'd like to raise the question of "how do we deepen the experience of ecotherapy?" In the prelude to Kellert and Wilson's classic volume, *Biophilia Hypothesis* (1993), Scott McVey quotes Loren Eisley: "One does not meet oneself until one catches the reflection in an eye other than human" (p. 8). Ecotherapy can help articulate the need to encounter the Other in order to more deeply know ourselves. Too often, our perspective of the Self is narrowed by culture and society. This seems especially true as so many people are heavily engaged with social media where the focus is almost exclusively on humans and human-made artifacts. When so much of our life energy is focused on screens and two-dimensional interactions, we narrow our experiences, our senses, and our perspective. To be fully alive, we need to experience the full range of our sensorial capacity outside of the human-dominated space. We need to experience the ecological Self, as we discussed in Chapter 5. By including the relationship an individual has with the natural world as part of our definition of well-being, we open the possibility of exploring that part of the Self. As clinicians, we recognize that deep therapeutic work can happen in that space. Intentional connections with nature—wild nature, nearby nature, backyard nature, furry pet nature—help one feel fully awake, fully engaged, and alive.

Meeting the client where they are in terms of their interactions with nature and supporting them in their engagement, or encouraging a client who is disconnected from nature to create engagement through a nature prescription, conveys the clinician's belief that a relationship with the natural world is a *necessity* of well-being. As Clinebell (1996) reminds us in his classic book, *Ecotherapy: Healing Ourselves,*

Healing the Earth, one of the rewards of developing an intimate bond with nature is celebrating those times when our own wildness is awakened by the wildness of nature. He refers to cultural historian, Thomas Berry, who observed that the outer world of nature activates the inner world. Berry went on to clarify that this relationship is not a subject–object relationship, but a subject–subject relationship—in other words, a relationship of reciprocity.

We need this dialectic of inner and outer landscapes for human flourishing. We need to be outdoors interacting with the natural world. Reciprocity between the wild in nature and the wild within offers knowledge and experience that only the wild can give us. Direct experiences of wild nature can produce the experiences of awe, spirit, enchantment, and a sense of the sacred—all of which are hard to articulate, define, and measure. But we *know it* when we experience it. In an essay I wrote for the journal *Ecopsychology* titled "How Deep Can We Go?" I pointed to wildness in the natural world and wildness within each of us as being at the heart of ecopsychology. I described wildness as that quality that makes each moment count when we feel fully alive and engaged; when we feel deep love for our child, or our lover, or nonhuman Other; when we feel humility in the face of awesome natural beauty, or vulnerability as part of the food chain; when we feel deep protectiveness for that which we love, human or otherwise; and when we feel a oneness with the universe (Hasbach, 2013).

As we narrow our life experiences and perspectives by being removed from nature and by being tethered to technology so much of the time, we not only diminish human flourishing, we also diminish our humanity and hinder human development. If we settle for only virtual nature interactions, we will see our reflection only in ourselves and our own creations. At a time of climate crisis, we need to tap into the wisdom of the natural world.

Making the Connection: Human Health and Planetary Health

Climate change is no longer something looming in the future—it is here. Climate change is an ongoing and pervasive factor in our lives, and it will continue to have global impact for the foreseeable future. In the last chapter, we discussed how the individual practitioner can address the chronic psychological impacts of climate change with their clients and patients. Here, we look at how climate-aware clinicians can leverage their knowledge and skill set to strengthen communities, give voice to social justice issues as they relate to climate change inequities, and engage the public on the topic.

But the reality is that it is not just climate change we are dealing with; it is change to the entire ecosystem we depend on for life. Many scientists believe we have entered a new geological era called the Anthropocene Era, characterized by human's deep and dramatic impact on the Earth's biophysical conditions. The formalization of the Anthropocene Era depends on whether the human effects on Earth are substantial enough to eventually appear in rock strata. Most scientists agree that human's impact on the Earth was relatively small prior to the Industrial Revolution. But advancements in technology since then have made it possible for humans to have widespread impact on many aspects of the Earth system. The emerging transdisciplinary field of Planetary Health focuses on analyzing and addressing the impacts of destabilized natural systems on human health and all life on Earth (Planetary Health Alliance, 2024).

An important resource for clinicians to be aware of is the Planetary Health Alliance, a consortium of more than 450 universities, nongovernmental organizations, research institutes, and government entities from more than 75 countries working together to understand and address global environmental change and its health impacts. The Planetary Health Alliance was founded in 2016 and was housed at Harvard University. Since November 2023, the Alliance has been headquartered at Johns Hopkins University at the Johns Hopkins Institute for Planetary Health. The mission of the alliance is, in part, to prepare communities for a comprehensive shift in how humans interact with each other and nature, in order to secure a livable future for humanity and the rest of life on Earth. With an emphasis on interdisciplinarity—working across disciplines—the alliance supports the dissemination of new research, the development of education materials, and the collaborations of various communities of practice around the world.

There are many avenues for involvement for the mental health clinician within the alliance including the Clinicians for Planetary Health (https://www.planetaryhealthalliance.org/clinicians-for-planetary-health) and an initiative called Connecting Climate Minds (https://www.planetaryhealthalliance.org/connecting-climate-minds). I encourage the reader to explore these options.

Though our health systems have made huge gains in public health, resulting in increased life expectancy and decreased child mortality, the Earth's ecological health is in decline. The Planetary Health Alliance summarizes what scientists call "the Great Acceleration" of human consumption patterns since 1950 that has contributed to the ecological decline. Here are a few highlights:

- The human population has increased nearly 200%
- Fossil fuel consumption has increased over 550%
- Fish removed from global waters has increased 350%
- We have dammed 60% of the Earth's rivers and cleared nearly half of the temperate and tropical forests
- We consume half of the accessible fresh water every year, and we currently use half of the Earth's livable surface to grow food

This Great Acceleration of human consumption patterns has had profound impacts on the natural systems of the Earth including:

- The atmospheric carbon dioxide levels have increased 24%
- The oceans have become 30% more acidic since the Industrial Revolution
- We are losing species at the unprecedented rate of 150 species per day including pollinators needed to grow plants and crops

These changes to the ecosystem are affecting human health. Scientists point to climate change, biodiversity loss, and deforestation as factors contributing to the emergence of intensely infectious diseases. Increased drought, loss of pollinators, and extreme weather events are factors contributing to crop failure. Air pollution contributes to cardiorespiratory illnesses. Climate-fueled weather events like hurricanes, drought, wildfires, and rising sea levels put people's lives at risk. These acute events and chronic concerns can have severe mental health consequences. As a profession, we need to be prepared to address the psychological implications of the environmental changes that are, and will continue to, affect us all.

With its emphasis on the human–nature relationship, ecopsychology sits at the heart of navigating the challenges we face and the profound changes we must make. As a field, ecopsychology focuses on how we can both enhance human well-being through nature interactions and become better stewards of nature, as we encourage a reciprocal relationship with the rest of the natural world. Other areas of psychology have important roles to play as well; environmental psychology, conservation psychology, and social psychology offer research and perspectives that are valuable and needed to address the complex issues we face. No one discipline can tackle the challenges ahead. Stepping out of our silos and collaborating with other health care professionals, community leaders, policy makers, city planners, and educators to raise awareness of the connection between human health and planetary health is essential.

Most mental health providers are unprepared to address the consequences of climate change and the impacts of planetary health decline. Just as training is needed to understand the benefits of the human–nature connection, training models must include how to help people navigate the acute and chronic stressors of climate change and the behavioral changes needed at the individual and societal levels. Professional organizations (e.g., American Psychological Association and American Counseling Association) are beginning to address these issues through their various task forces that focus on advocacy efforts and curriculum competencies.

Health professionals and mental health clinicians have a unique role in influencing clients, patients, policy makers, and the public on making the connection between human health and planetary health. As mentioned earlier, research shows that people look to their health care professionals for guidance on how to navigate climate change. The complex relationship of human health and planetary health is an extension of these deeply felt concerns. In the APA and ecoAmerica 2021 report titled "Mental Health and Our Changing Climate:

Impacts, Inequities, Responses" (Clayton, Manning et al.), opportunities are outlined for mental health professionals to elevate their climate leadership. I encourage the reader to review the full report. Here, I summarize and add my thoughts to what mental health professionals can do to extend their role to motivate engagement and action on climate solutions beyond the clinical work we do with our individual clients and patients.

1. *Educate yourself.* Become aware of the issues of climate change and the connections between human health and planetary health and the mental health impacts they can produce. Stay current on climate news including local projects and initiatives in your community.

2. *Climate leadership can involve reaching out to other mental health colleagues.* They may be just as concerned. Engage in discussions on the topic and share ideas, current research, and best practices. Offer a presentation or workshop at a regional or national conference.

3. *Reach out to other health professionals in your community.* Practice stepping outside the silo of the profession and engage with other health care providers to bring attention to the impacts of climate change. Those working with children and families may be especially interested in engaging the topic.

4. *Connect with your professional organizations.* Many professional mental health organizations have public statements, policies, and established committees or divisions focused on addressing climate change including the American Psychological Association, the American Psychiatric Association, the American Counseling Association, and others. Engage with these organizations to strengthen statements, programs, education, and advocacy. These associations also offer the opportunity for collaborations between researchers and practitioners—essential for creating accessible and effective tools for clinical practice.

5. *Be a visible and vocal leader in your spheres of influence.* Professionals in the mental health community have

a respected platform to influence the dialogue on climate change, heighten awareness of the relationship between climate change and mental health, and contribute to policies and healthy climate solutions. Clinicians can encourage climate preparedness and prevention at the personal and community levels. Consider submitting an article or an op-ed on the topic to newspapers, radio, social media, blogs, and TV outlets. Collaborate with colleagues and climate advocates to influence policy design and outcomes.

6. *Green your practice.* Institute programs and practices in your organization or office practice to reduce your climate impact.

Our well-being and that of future generations depend on a healthy planet. Climate-aware practitioners understand that the issues of climate change and planetary health are not only determinants for physical health, but also for mental health. Clinicians have a role to play in addressing climate-related concerns of their clients and patients and in advocating, educating, and participating in the development of climate solutions beyond the therapy office. Nature-informed clinicians are in a position to become highly visible leaders, working to achieve positive outcomes in the micro level of the therapeutic environment and by influencing key policy areas based on the outcomes at the macro level (Burls, 2007).

Clinicians have the skills to help reframe people's perspectives from seeing climate change as a threat, which can lead to a fight, flight, freeze reaction, to seeing it as a challenge, which opens the possibilities for collaborations and creative solutions. Ecotherapists acknowledge that we are intimately connected with the environment and each other. We can use our skills to invite people to wake up from the delusion that we are separate from nature and encourage people to fully engage in a *reciprocal* relationship with the natural world.

CONCLUSION

In this book, I offer an overview of the practice of ecotherapy that is grounded in the tenets of ecopsychology, evolutionary psychology, and biophilia and recognizes and values the ecological context of human life. I presented research that provides evidence that interactions between humans and the rest of nature are *essential* for our mental and physical health. I suggested practices and methods for working with clients and patients that include nature as a partner in the therapeutic process—through mindfully creating restorative environments in one's office, moving therapy sessions outdoors, and writing nature prescriptions to encourage direct interactions with the natural world. I introduced the concept of therapeutic nature language as a tool to begin to systematically think about interaction patterns between humans and nature and offered ways to incorporate such patterns into clinical work. I discussed the mental health impacts of our changing planet and looked at how the climate-aware clinician might address patient concerns and contribute to healthy climate solutions. Finally, I offered possible future directions for the field of ecopsychology and the practice of ecotherapy.

Writing this book has been a labor of love and a reflection of my therapeutic work with patients over the last three decades. I have seen firsthand the impact of nature partnership in the outcomes of many patients' therapeutic journeys. I've heard patients reflect on the joy they experience in feeling they are embedded in something bigger than themselves and that they belong. I've heard a former drug addict say that he didn't realize he could experience sustained happiness and a sense of peace until he "found nature." I've seen couples communicate and reconnect in healthier ways after working on a community restoration project together. I've listened to a patient describe the cycles of her garden as she worked through the grief of the death of her husband. I've seen the balance that time in nature offers to many who are overly connected to their digital devices. I witnessed the companionship and love a little dog brought to a man who had lost his wife. I've sat with couples as they wrestled with profound decisions like whether to start a family in light of the current state of the environment. I've seen a community come together in an outdoor ritual to help one another after a devastating wildfire. These are just a small sample of the stories I've been privileged to share in with my patients. As a clinician, you have stories of your own. It is my hope that this book provides clinicians with a solid foundation in the theories and practices of ecotherapy, so that ecotherapy can stand alongside other major therapies, to be drawn on when it promises effective treatment and be incorporated seamlessly into a traditional therapeutic practice.

Finally, I hope that as we come to more fully appreciate the *necessity* of nature in our lives, we engage in a truly reciprocal relationship with the natural world—one where as humans, we engage in pro-environmental behaviors to protect nature, to nurture the Other, and to grow as a species so that we can authentically recognize our responsibility to future generations of humans and the more-than-human world.

REFERENCES

Albrecht, G. (2012). Psychoterratic conditions in a scientific and technological world. In P. H. Kahn & P. H. Hasbach (Eds.), *Ecopsychology: Science, totems, and the technological species* (pp. 241–264). MIT Press.

American Counseling Association. (2014). *2014 code of ethics.* Retrieved from https://www.counseling.org/docs/default-source/default-document-library/ethics/2014-aca-code-of-ethics.pdf

American Psychological Association. (2017). *Ethical principles of psychologists and code of conduct* (2002, amended effective June 1, 2010, and January 1, 2017). Retrieved from https://www.apa.org/ethics/code/

American Psychological Association. (2020, February 6). *Majority of US adults believe climate change is most important issue today* [Press release]._https://www.apa.org/news/press/releases/2020/02/climate-change

Atchley, R. A., Strayer, D. L., & Atchley, P. (2012). Creativity in the wild: Improving creative reasoning through immersion in natural settings. *PLOS ONE, 7*(12), e51474. https://doi.org/10.1371/journal.pone.005147

Ballew, M. T., & Omoto, A. M. (2018). Absorption: How nature experiences promote awe and other positive emotions. *Ecopsychology, 19*(1), 26–35. https://doi.org/10.1089/eco.2017.0044

Balling, J. D., & Falk, J. H. (1982). Development of visual preference for natural environments. *Environment and Behavior, 14,* 5–38.

Beck, A. M., & Katcher, A. H. (1996). *Between pets and people: The importance of animal companionship.* Purdue University Press.

Beck, A. M., & Meyers, N. M. (1996). Health enhancement and companion animal ownership. *Annual Review of Public Health, 17,* 247–257.

Berry, T. (1988). *The dream of the earth.* Sierra Club Books

Berman, M. G., Jonides, J., & Kaplan, S. (2008). The cognitive benefits of interacting with nature. *Psychological Science, 19,* 1207–1212.

Berto, R. (2005). Exposure to restorative environments helps restore attentional capacity. *Journal of Environmental Psychology, 25,* 249–259.

Boyd, F., White, M., Bell, S., & Burt, J. (2018). Who doesn't visit natural environments for recreation and why: A population representative analysis of spatial, individual and temporal factors among adults in England. *Landscape and Urban Planning* (vol. 175, pp. 102–113). https://doi.org/10.1016/j.landurbplan.2018.03.016

Bratman, G. N., Hamilton, J. P., & Daily, G. C. (2012). The impacts of nature experience on human cognitive function and mental health. *Annuals of the New York Academy of Science, 1249*, 118–136. https://doi.org/10.1111/j .1749-6632.2011.06400.x

Bratman, G. N., Hamilton, J. P., Hahn, K. S., Daily, G. C., & Gross, J. J. (2015). Nature experience reduces rumination and subgenual prefrontal cortex activation. *PNAS, 112*, 8567–8572. https://doi.org/10.1073/pnas.1510459112

Bratman, G. N., Anderson, C. B., Berman, M. G., Cochran, B., DeVries, S., Flanders, J., Folke, C., Frumkin, H., Gross, J. J., Hartig, T., Kahn, P. H. Jr., Kuo, M., Lawler, J. J., Levin, P. S., Lindahl, T., Meyer-Lindenberg, A., Mitchell, R., Ouyang, Z., Roe, J. Scarlett, L., . . . Daily, G. C. (2019). Nature and mental health: An ecosystem service perspective. *Science Advances, 5*(7). https://doi.org/10.1126/sciadv.aax0903

Bratman, G. N., Olvera-Alvarez, H. A., & Gross, J. J. (2021). The affective benefits of nature exposure. *Social and Personality Psychology Compass, 15*(8). https://doi.org.10.1111/spc3.12630

Burls, A. (2007). People and green spaces: promoting public health and mental well-being through ecotherapy. *Journal of Public Mental Health, 6*(3), 24–39. https://doi.org/10.1108/17465729200700018

Buttel, L., Kobayashi, N. M., Kobayashi, N. P., Lake, C., Logan, D., Speiser, M., & Voss, J. (2020). American Climate Perspectives Survey 2020, Vol. II: Americans may feel isolated in their climate concern. EcoAmerica and Lake Research Partners.

Buzzell, L., & Chalquist, C. (Eds.). (2009). *Ecotherapy: Healing with nature in mind*. Sierra Club Books.

Cambridge University Press. (n.d.). Ritual. In *Cambridge dictionary*. Retrieved August 18, 2024. from https://dictionary.cambridge.org/dictionary/ english/ritual

Clayton, S. (2020). Climate anxiety: Psychological responses to climate change. *Journal of Anxiety Disorders, 74*(8), 102263. https://doi.org/10.1016/j .janxdis.2020.102263

Clayton, S., Czellar, S., Nartova-Bochaver, S., Skibins, J. C., Salazar, G., Tseng, Y., Irkhin, B., & Monge-Rodriguez, F. S. (2021). Cross-cultural validation of a revised Environmental Identity Scale. *Sustainability, 13*, 2387. https://doi.org/10.3390/su13042387

Clayton, S., Manning, C. M., Speiser, M., & Hill, A. N. (2021). Mental health and our changing climate: Impacts, inequities, responses. American Psychological Association and ecoAmerica.

Clayton, S., & Opotow, S. (2003). *Identity and the natural environment*. MIT Press.

Clinebell, H. (1996). *Ecotherapy: Healing ourselves, healing the earth*. Fortress Press.

Conn, S. A. (1998). Living in the Earth: Ecopsychology, health and psychotherapy. *The Humanistic Psychologist, 26*(1–3), 179198. https://doi.org/10.1080/08873267.1998.9976972

Costello, A., Abbas, M., Allen, A., Ball, S., Bell, S., Bellamy, R., Friel, S., Groce, N., Johnson, A., Kett, M., Lee, M., Levy, C., Maslin, M., McCoy, D., McGuire, B., Montgomery, H., Napier, D., Pagel, C., Patel, J., Puppim de Oliveira, J.A., Redclift, N., Rees, H., Rogger, D., Scott, J., Stephenson, J., Twigg, J., Wolff, J., Patterson, C. (2009, May 16). Managing the health effects of climate change. *The Lancet, 373*(9676), 1693–1733. doi: 10.1016/S0140-6736(09)60935-1

Cunsolo, A., Harper, S. L., Minor, K., Hayes, K., Williams, K. G., & Howard, C. (2020). Ecological grief and anxiety: The start of a healthy response to climate change? *The Lancet Planetary Health, 4*(7), 261–263. https://doi.org/10.1016/S2542-5196(20)30144-3

Earle, S. A. (1995). *Sea change: A message of the oceans*. Ballantine Books.

Foster, S., & Little, M. (1997). *The roaring of the sacred river: The wilderness quest for vision and self-healing*. Lost Borders Press.

Fox, W. (1995). The deep ecology-Ecofeminism debate and its parallels. In G. Sessions (Ed.), *Deep ecology for the 21ˢᵗ century* (pp. 269–289). Shambhala Publications.

Frumkin, H. (2012). Building the science base: Ecopsychology meets clinical epidemiology. In P. H. Kahn & P. H. Hasbach (Eds.), *Ecopsychology: Science, totems, and the technological species* (pp.141–172). MIT Press.

Frumkin, H., Bratman, G. N., Breslow, S., Cochran, B., Kahn, P. H. Jr, Lawler, J. J., Levin, P. S., Tandon, P. S., Varanasi, U., Wolf, K. L., & Wood, S. A. (2017). Nature contact and human health: A research agenda. *Environmental Health Perspectives, 25*(7), 1–18. https://doi.org/10.1289/EHP1663

Gray, D., Hewlett, D., Hammon, J., & Aburrow, S. (2024). (Re)Connecting with nature: Exploring nature-based interventions for psychological health and wellbeing. In: N. Finneran, D. Hewlett, & R. Clarke (Eds.), *Managing protected areas* (pp. 143–166). Palgrave Macmillan. https://doi.org/10.1007/978-3-031-40783-3_9

Hasbach, P. H. (2012). Ecotherapy. In P. H. Kahn & P. H. Hasbach (Eds.) *Ecopsychology: Science, totems, and the technological species* (115–139). MIT Press.

Hasbach, P. H. (2013). How deep can we go? *Ecopsychology, 5*(4), 228–230. https://doi.org/10.1089/eco.2013.0057

Hasbach, P. H. (2015). Therapy in the face of climate change. *Ecopsychology, 7*(4), 205–210. https://doi.org/10.1089/eco.2015.0018

Hasbach, P. H. (2016). Prescribing nature: techniques, challenges, and ethical considerations. In M. Jordon & J. Hinds (Eds.), *Ecotherapy: Theory research & practice* (pp. 138–147). Palgrave.

Hedlund-De Witt, A. (2013). Pathways to environmental responsibility: A qualitative exploration of the spiritual dimension of nature experience. *Journal for the Study of Religion, Nature and Culture, 7*, 154–186. https://doi.org/10.1558/jsrnc.v7i2.154

Heerwagen, J. (1990). The psychological aspects of windows and window design. In K. H. Anthony, J. Choi, & B. Orland (Eds.), *Proceedings of the 21st annual conference of the Environmental Design Research Association* (pp. 269–280). EDRA.

Hickman, C., Marks, E., Pihkala, P., Clayton, S., Lewandowski, R. E., Mayali, E. E., Wray, B., Mellor, C., & Van Susteren, L. (2021). Climate anxiety in children and young people and their beliefs about government responses to climate change: A global survey. *The Lancet Planetary Health 2021, 5*(12), e863–e873. https://doi.org/10.1016/S2542-5196(21)00278-3

Hinds, J., & Sparks, P. (2009). Investigating environmental identity, well-being, and meaning. *Ecopsychology, 1,* 181–186. https://doi.org/10.1089/eco.2009.0026

Howie, L. D., Pastor, P. N., & Lukacs, S. L. (2014, April). Use of medication prescribed for emotional or behavioral difficulties among children aged 6–17 years in the United States, 2011–2012. *NCHS Data Brief, 148*, 1–8. PMID: 24762418.

Jung, C. G. (1984). *Dream analysis: Notes of the seminars given in 1928–1930.* Princeton University Press.

Jung, C. G. (1957/ 1989*). Memories, dreams, reflections*. Vintage Books.

Kahn, P. H., & Hasbach, P. H. (2012). *Ecopsychology: Science, totems, and the technological species.* MIT Press.

Kahn, P. H., & Hasbach, P. H. (2013). *The rediscovery of the wild.* MIT Press.

Kahn, P. H., Ruckert, J. H., & Hasbach, P. H. (2012). A nature language. In P. H. Kahn & P. H. Hasbach (Eds.), *Ecopsychology: Science, totems, and the technological species.* MIT Press.

Kaplan, S. (1995). The restorative benefits of nature: toward an integrative framework. *Journal of Environmental Psychology, 15*, 169–182.

Kellert, S. R., & Wilson, E. O. (1993). *The biophilia hypothesis.* Island Press.

Kellert, S. R. (2002). Experiencing nature: Affective, cognitive, and evaluative development in children. In P. H. Kahn & S. R. Kellert (Eds.) *Children and nature: Psychological, Sociocultural, and evolutionary investigations.*(pp. 117–152). MIT Press

Kellert, S. R. (2012). *Birthright: People and nature in the modern world.* Yale University Press.

Lakeoff, G., & Johnson, M. (1981). *Metaphors we live by.* University of Chicago Press.

La Puma, J. (2019). Nature therapy: An essential prescription for health. *Alternative and Complementary Therapies, 25*(2), 1–4. https://doi.org/10.1089/act2019.29209.jlp

La Puma, J. (2023, Feb. 8). What is nature-based medicine and what does it do? *American Journal of Lifestyle Medicine, 17*(4). https://doi.org/10.1177/15598276221148395

Leong, L. Y. C., Fischer, R., & McClure, J. (2014). Are nature lovers more innovative? The relationship between connectedness with nature and cognitive styles. *Journal of Environmental Psychology, 40,* 57–63. https://doi.org/10.1016/j.jenvp.2014.03.007

Lopez, B., & Gwartney, D. (2006). *Home ground: Language for an American landscape.* Trinity University Press.

Louv, R. (2008). *Last child in the woods: Saving our children from nature-deficit disorder.* Algonquin Books of Chapel Hill.

Louv, R. (2019). *Our wild calling: How connecting with animals can transform our lives—and save theirs.* Algonquin Books of Chapel Hill.

Marcus, C. C., & Barnes, M. (1999). *Healing gardens: Therapeutic benefits and design recommendations.* John Wiley & Sons.

Maslow, A. H. (1974). *Religions, values, and peak experiences.* Viking Press.

Mayer, F. S., & Franz, C. M. (2004). The Connectedness to Nature Scale: A measure of individuals' feeling in community with nature. *Journal of Environmental Psychology, 24,* 503–515.

Millikin, J. W., & Johnson, S. M. (2000). Telling tales: Disquisitions in emotionally focused therapy. *Journal of Family Psychotherapy, 11,* 73–79.

Moore, E. O. (1981). A prison environment's effect on health care service demands. *Journal of Environmental Systems, 11,* 17–34.

Moxley, E. (2022, March 7). Green space and heart health: What's the connection? Preventive Cardiovascular Nurses Association. https://pcna.net/author/elizabethmoxley/

Nadkarni, N. M., Hasbach, P. H., Thys, T., Crockett, E. G., & Schnacker, L. (2017). Impacts of nature imagery on people in severely nature-deprived environments. *Frontiers in Ecology and the Environment, 15*(7), 395–403. https://doi.org/10.1002/fee.1518

Naess, A. (1995). The deep ecological movement–some philosophical aspects. In G. Sessions (Ed.), *Deep ecology for the 21ˢᵗ century* (pp. 64–84). Shambhala Publications.

National Association of Social Workers (2021). *NASW Code of Ethics*. Retrieved from https://www.socialworkers.org/About/Ethics/Code-of-Ethics

National Oceanic and Atmospheric Association. (2024). 2023 was the world's warmest year on record, by far. Retrieved from https://www.noaa.gov/news/2023-was-worlds-warmest-year-on-record-by-far

National Oceanic and Atmospheric Administration. (2022). *National Bird Day*. https://oceanservice.noaa.gov/ecosystems/estuaries/bird-watching.html

Neale, C., Aspinall, P., Roe, J., Tilley, S., Mavros, P., Cinderby, S., Coyne, R., Thin, N., & Ward Thompson, C. (2020). The impact of walking in different urban environments on brain activity in older people, *Cities & Health, 4*(1), 94–106. https://doi.org/10.1080/23748834.2019.1619893

Nhat Hanh, T. (1991). *Peace in every step: The path of mindfulness in everyday life.* Bantam Books.

Nisbet, E. K., Zelenski, J. M., & Murphy, S. A. (2011). Happiness is in our nature: Exploring nature relatedness as a contributor to subjective well-being. *Journal of Happiness Studies, 12*(2), 303–322. https://doi.org/10.1007/s10902-010-9197-7

Office of the U. S. Surgeon General. (2023). *Our epidemic of loneliness and isolation: The U.S. surgeon general's advisory on the healing effects of social contact and community.* Retrieved from https://www.hhs.gov/sites/default/files/surgeon-general-social-connection-advisory.pdf

Orchin, I. (2004). In consultation: Taking therapy outdoors. *Psychotherapy Networker, 28.* Retrieved from http://www.midlifefrontiers.com/psychotherapy/docs/NetworkerPublishedPiece.pdf

Oregon Department of Transportation. (2022). *2020 Labor Day wildfires hazard tree and debris removal operations after action report.* Retrieved from https://digitalcollections.library.oregon.gov/nodes/view/208693

Orr, D. (1991). *Ecological literacy.* State University of New York Press.

Orr, D. (2009). Forward. In L. Buzzell & C. Chalquist (Eds.), *Ecotherapy: Healing with nature in mind.* Sierra Club Books.

Oxford University Press. (n.d.). Nature. In *Oxford English Dictionary.* Retrieved from https://www.oed.com/search/dictionary/?scope=Entries&q=nature

Park, B., Tsunetsugu, T., Kasetani, T., Hirano, H., Kagawa, T., Sato, M., & Miyazaki, Y. (2007). Physiological effects of Shinrin-yoku (taking in the atmosphere of the forest)–using salivary cortisol and cerebral activity as indicators. *Journal of Physiological Anthropology, 26*, 123–128. https://doi.org/10.2114/jpa2.26.123

Park, S. H., & Mattson, R. H. (2009). Therapeutic influences of plants in hospital rooms on surgical recovery, *HortScience, 44*(1), 1–4.

Pitt, C., Norris, K., & Pecl, G. (2024). Informing future directions for climate anxiety interventions: A mixed-method study of professional perspectives. *Journal of Outdoor and Environmental Education, 27*, 209–234. https://doi.org/10.1007/s42322-023-00156-y

Planetary Health Alliance. (2024). Retrieved from https://www.planetary healthalliance.org/home-page

Plotkin, B. (2003). *Soulcraft: Crossing into the mysteries of nature and psyche.* New World Library.

Pyle, R. M. (1993). *The thunder tree: Lessons from an urban wildland.* Houghton Mifflin.

Richardson, M., Hamlin, I., Butler, C. W., Thomas, R., & Hunt, A. (2022). Actively noticing nature (not just time in nature) helps promote nature connectedness. *Ecopsychology, 14*(1). https://doi.org/10.1089/eco.2021.0023

Rideout, V. J., Foehr, U. G., & Roberts, D. F. (2010). Generation M2: Media in the lives of 8–18-year-olds. Henry J. Kaiser Family Foundation. Retrieved from http://www.kff.org/other/report/generation-m2-media-in-the-lives-of-8-to-18-year-olds/

Rodrigues, M. (2024). Climate scientists grapple with mental exhaustion. *Nature, 632*, 695–697. https://doi.org/10.1038/d41586-024-02605-0

Roe, J., Aspinall, P., Mavros, P., & Coyne, R. (2013). Engaging the brain: The impact of natural versus urban scenes using novel EEG methods in an experimental setting. *Journal of Environmental Science, 1*(2), 93–104.

Roszak, T. (1992). *The voice of the earth: An exploration of ecopsychology.* Simon & Schuster.

Roszak, T., Gomes, M., & Kanner, A. (1995). *Ecopsychology: Restoring the earth, healing the mind.* Sierra Club Books.

Schreiber, M. (2021, March). Addressing climate change concerns in practice. *Monitor on Psychology.* American Psychological Association.

Schroeder, H. W. (1992). The spiritual aspect of nature: A perspective from depth psychology. In: G. A. Vander Stoep (Ed.). Proceedings of the 1991 Northeastern Recreation Research Symposium; 1991 April 7-9; Saratoga Springs, NY. Gen. Tech. Rep. NE-160. Radnor, PA: U.S. Department of Agriculture, Forest Service, Northeastern Forest Experiment Station: 25–30.

Schroeder, H. (2012). Giving voice to the experiential value of natural environments. *The Humanistic Psychologist, 40*, 136–152.

Schultz, P., Shriver. C., Tabanico, J. J., & Khazian, A. M. (2004). Implicit connections with nature. *Journal of Environmental Psychology, 24,* 31–42. https://doi.org/10.1016/s0272-4944(03)00022-7

Selhub, E. M., & Logan, A. C. (2012). *Your brain on nature.* John Wiley & Sons Canada.

Sexton, T. L., & Stanton, M. (2016). Systems theories. In J. C. Norcross, G. R. VandenBos, D. K. Freedheim, & B. O. Olatunji (Eds.), *APA handbook of clinical psychology: Theory and research* (pp. 213–239). American Psychological Association. https://doi.org/10.1037/14773-008

Shepard, P. (1998). *Coming home to the Pleistocene.* Island Press.

Soga, M., Gaston, K. J., & Yamaura, Y. (2016). Gardening is beneficial for health: A meta-analysis. *Preventive Medicine Reports, 5,* 92–99. https://doi .org/10.1016/j.pmedr2016.11.007

Speiser, M., & Ishaq, M. (July, 2024). Americans voice a clear call for health professionals to lead on climate. *American Climate Perspective Survey 2024, Vol II.* ecoAmerica.

Stryer, S. B. (2024). Using nature prescriptions to reconnect people with the outdoors and improve health and wellbeing. *American Journal of Health Promotion, 38*(1), 140–142. https://doi.org/10.1177/08901171231210806d

Substance Abuse and Mental Health Services Administration. (2022). Key substance use and mental health indicators in the United States: Results from the 2021 National Survey on Drug Use and Health (HHS Publication No. PEP22-07-01-005, NSDUH Series H-57). Rockville, MD: Center for Behavioral Health Statistics and Quality, Substance Abuse and Mental Health Services Administration. Retrieved from https://www.samhsa.gov/ data/report/2021-nsduh-annual-national-report .

Tarnas, R. (1993). *The passion of the western mind: Understanding the ideas that have shaped our world view.* Ballantine Books.

Tate, W., Chawla, L., Sachs, A. L., Litt, J. S., & Razani, N. (2024). Nature prescribing or nature programming? Complementary practices to increase time in nature to support mental health. *Ecopsychology, 16*(4). https://doi .org/10.1089/eco.2023.0064

Tempest Williams, T. (2001). *Red.* Pantheon Books.

Ulrich, R. S. (1983). Aesthetic and affective response to natural environment. *Human Behavior Environmental Advanced Theory Res., 6,* 85–125.

Ulrich, R. S. (1984). View through a window may influence recovery from surgery. *Science, 224,* 420–421.

Ulrich, R. (2001). Effects of interior design on wellness: Theory and recent scientific research. *Journal of Healthcare Interior Design,* 97–109.

Ulrich, R. S., & Gilpin, L. (2003). Healing arts: Nutrition for the soul. In S. B.

Frampton, L. Gilpin, & P. A. Charmel (Eds.), *Putting patients first: Designing and practicing patient-centered care* (pp. 117–146). John Wiley & Sons.

Ulrich, R. S., Simons, R., Losito, B., Fiorito, E., Miles, M., & Zelson, M. (1991). Stress recovery during exposure to natural and urban environments. *Journal of Environmental Psychology, 11*(3), 201–230.

Wagener, A. E. (2017). Metaphor in professional counseling. *The Professional Counselor, 7*(2), 144–154). https://doi.org/10.1524/aew.7.2.144

Wang, H., Safer, D. L., Cosentino, M., Cooper, R., Van Susteren, L., Coren, E., Nosek, G., Lertzman, R., & Sutton, S. (2023). Coping with eco-anxiety: An interdisciplinary perspective for collective learning and strategic communication. *Journal of Climate Change and Health, 9*, 100211. https://doi.org/10.1016/j.joclim2023.100211

Ward Thompson, C., Aspinall, P., Roe, J., Robertson, L., & Miller, D. (2016). Mitigating stress and supporting health in deprived urban communities: The importance of green space and the social environment. *International journal of environmental research and public health, 13*(4), 440. https://doi.org/10.3390/ijerph13040440

Williams, F. (2016, January). This is your brain on nature. *National Geographic.*

Yeager, R., Riggs, D. W., DeJarnett, N., Tollerud, D. J., Wilson, J., Conklin, D. J., O'Toole, T. E., McCracken, J., Lorkiewicz, P., Zhengzhi, X., Zafar, N., Krishnasamy, S., Srivastava, S., Finch, J., Keith, R., De Filippis, A., Rai, S. N., Liu, G., & Bhatnagar, A. (2018). Association between residential greenness and cardiovascular disease risk. *Journal of the American Heart Association, 7*(24). https://doi.org/10.1161/JAHA.118.009117

Yin, J., Yuan, J., Arfaei, N., Catalano, P. J., Allen, J. G., & Spengler, J. D. (2020). Effects of biophilic environment on stress and anxiety recovery: A between-subjects experiment in virtual reality. *Environment International, 136*, 1–10.

Zarr, R., Cottreil, L., & Merrill, C. (2017). Park prescription (DC Park Rx): A new strategy to combat chronic disease in children. *Journal of Physical Activity & Health, 14,* 1–2.

Zelenski, J. M. & Nisbet, E. K. (2014). Happiness and feeling connected: the distinct role of nature relatedness. *Environment and Behavior, 4*(1), 3–23.

INDEX

Note: Italicized page locators refer to figures.

cognitive-behavioral therapy, ecotherapy
methods combined with, 6, 83
cognitive functioning
nature contact and, 42
nature walk report on, 22–23
three-day effect and, 36
collaborative research on nature and well-
being, need for, 147
collective unconscious, ecological unconscious and, 23, 30, 136
Coming Home to the Pleistocene (Shepard),
56
compatibility, natural environments and, 45
competency
ecopsychology field and, 116
outdoor therapy and, 113, 114, 116–17
confidentiality, outdoor therapy and, 79
80, 113, 114–15
Conn, S., 58
Connectedness to Nature Scale (CNS),
63–64
Connecting Climate Minds, 152
connection, felt sense and, 27–28. *see also*
belonging, sense of
conservation biology, nature language
and, 99
conservation psychology
conservation psychology, relationship
with ecopsychology and environmental psychology, 16, *17*, 153
contemplative nature walk exercise, 93
contexts of care, expanded, 35, *35*, 57
Cooper, R., 128
cosmic evolution, ecological unconscious
and, 247
cosmic history, ecological unconscious
and, 136
cosmology, paradigms and, 57
counterculture movement (1960s), modern
environmental movement and, 15
couples work
climate-aware clinicians and, 142
environment and impact on, 38
reconnection through nature in, 157–58

courtyard traditions, in hospitals, 40
COVID-19 pandemic, 23, 130
forest bathing during, 121
nature interactions and coping with, 147
creativity
environmental identity and, 54
nature experiences and, 34
crop failure, extreme weather events and,
152
cultural/social influences, in contexts of
care, 34, *35*
culture, worldviews and, 57

dams, ecological impact of, 152
David Suzuki Foundation 30x30 Nature
Challenge, 94
deep ecology
ecological unconscious and, 18, 23–25
ecopsychology and, 15
deep listening, 70
deforestation, 152
dementia, gardening and reduced risk
of, 147
Denmark, medical education in nature-
based medicine in, 86
dental offices
biophilic design and, 41
natural scenes mural study, 21–22, 75
depression, 10, 14, 147
climate change and planetary concerns
and, 59, 69, 132
lack of nature connectedness and, 85
loneliness and, 66
natural disasters and, 135
nature interactions and reduction in,
82, 145, 146, 147
rising rates of, 141
despair, young people and, 38
diabetes, 10, 85
*Diagnostic and Statistical Manual of Men-
tal Disorders (DSM-5-TR)*, 33
climate-related conditions in, need for,
148
individualistic orientation in, 58

digital devices, balancing time in nature
with use of, 158
digital technology
children and time spent with, asking
about, 143
increased presence and impact of, 17
see also social media
Diom, B., 95
direct attention capacity, restoring, natural environments and, 44–45, 64
directed attention fatigue, recovery from,
44, 45
disquisition, purpose of, 108
diverse populations, care farms and,
120–21
documentation, outdoor therapy and,
80–81, 114
dogs, in animal-assisted therapy, 118, 119
domestic violence, natural disasters and,
136
Dream Analysis (Jung), 8
droughts, 18, 135, 152

Earle, S., 55
earth
decline of ecological health on, 152
intrapsychic processes tied to, 136
earth elements, for ritual space, 105
earthquakes, 42
ecoAmerica, 11
American Climate Perspectives Survey,
137–38
American Psychological Association
collaboration, 11, 138, 153–54
climate change survey, 134
ecoanxiety, 18, 137, 138
contexts of care and, 35
definitions of, 11, 134
experiences of, 139
natural disasters and, 136
self-silencing and, 139
see also anxiety; climate change
ecofeminism, 15
eco-genogram, 54, 60–62, *61*

eco-history interview, 54, 60
ecological context, in contexts of care,
35, *35*
ecological perspectives, health-promotion
initiatives and, 146
ecological Self, 13, 55
active noticing and, 65
ecotherapy and, 37
experiencing, need for, 149
exploration of and validation for, 67
gray whale encounter and, 54, 58, 67
in practice, 65–67
see also environmental identity
ecological system, adding to scope of
treatment, 37–38
ecological unconscious, 7, 18, 23–25,
136
ethical responsibility to the planet and,
137
repression of *vs.* open access to,
136–37
ecoparalysis, 137
ecopsychology, 135, 144, 157
brief historical overview of, 15–17
central assumption of, 15
coining of term for, 15
competency issues and, 116–17
definition of, 14–15
emerging field of, 6
emphasis on human-nature relationship in, 153
growing interest in field of, 5
holistic perspective of, 58
introduction of, 33
practice of ecotherapy *vs.* theory of, 16
relationship with conservation psychology and environmental psychology, 16, *17,* 153
relevance of, 17–18
systems theory and, 34
wildness at heart of, 150
see also ecopsychology, five tenets
related to ecotherapy
Ecopsychology (journal), 150

ABOUT THE AUTHOR

A pioneer in the practice of ecotherapy, **Patricia H. Hasbach, PhD,** is a licensed psychotherapist, consultant, author, and college educator. In private practice for three decades, Dr. Hasbach offers traditional therapy and ecotherapy to adults, couples, families, and groups. Areas of specialty include managing anxiety and depression, relationship issues, parenting concerns, life transitions, environmental issues, and fostering health and wellness. She consults with hospitals, schools, businesses, correctional facilities, and community groups. Dr. Hasbach is the former codirector of the Ecopsychology Certificate Program in the Graduate School of Education and Counseling at Lewis & Clark College where she taught for 13 years. She sits on the editorial board of the peer-reviewed journal *Ecopsychology.*

Dr. Hasbach is the author of *Grounded: A Guided Journal to Help You Connect with the Power of Nature and Yourself* (2022), published by Simon & Schuster; and an author and coeditor of *The Rediscovery of the Wild* (2013) and *Ecopsychology: Science, Totems, and the Technological Species* (2012), published by MIT Press. She has published several book chapters in edited volumes and peer-reviewed articles in professional journals.

Her work has appeared in numerous popular outlets including *Time Magazine, Vogue, Outside Magazine, Sierra Magazine, The Smithsonian, Popular Science, The Christian Science Monitor, National Geographic, The New York Times, The Wall Street Journal, The Washington Post,* and *Metro UK.* In addition to several online blogs and podcasts, her work has been featured in professional outlets including

The Psychotherapy Networker, Counseling Today, Monitor on Psychology, APS Observer, and *Healthline.*

In her free time, she enjoys traveling, hiking, kayaking, gardening, and spending time with friends and family in nature. She lives with her husband and two pups on the McKenzie River near Eugene, Oregon.